GW01368244

ISBN-13: 978-1537410067

ISBN-10: 1537410067

Images by ananaline / Shutterstock

Book design by Rachel Shillcock

Editing by Kris Emery

Page 149 – 12 Angry Men written by Reginald Rose

Dear Gail
Best Wishes
Barbara

THE BOSS HAT

Barbara Nixon

DEDICATION

To Mum and John

CONTENTS

"   "

To be yourself in a world that is constantly trying to make you something else is the greatest accomplishment

– Ralph Waldo Emerson

INTRODUCTION

You're reading this because you're ready to be a *different* kind of Boss. The type of Boss who isn't a clone of someone else, who doesn't fit perfectly into a mould. A Boss who's ready to embrace their unique style.

To you, being a Boss isn't just about a job title or doing a job. It's about being true to yourself. It's about people. It's about growth, achieving potential and bringing the very best out of your team. And in turn bringing the very best out of yourself.

You're aware that a great Boss can achieve amazing results from the people they work with, and that just because we have to work every day doesn't mean that we have to sell our souls to do it. You know your teams spend more time with you then they do with their own families, and that you have the power to motivate, inspire, and help them grow so they can leave work at the end of the day with as much energy as they started and a glow that they've made a difference.

A great Boss, just like a great teacher, will support others to grow and succeed. A great Boss will *never* be forgotten.

You're reading this because you're ready to step up and be that person. You're ready to throw your old Boss Hat in the ring… and create a brand new one, one that fits a brand new you.

Welcome to the start of your Boss Hat journey.

"Only the truth of who you are, if realised, will set you free"

– Eckhart Tolle

ABOUT THIS BOOK

So, what do you call yourself? A manager? A leader? A business owner? A director? A CEO? The list goes on really. In fact, it doesn't even matter. In this book, I'm calling you a Boss. With a capital 'B'. You see, it's easier that way – just a neutral term for someone who leads a team. Similar to the word 'gaffa' (as my dad used to say) or 'Guv'nor'.

But what does it mean to me?

Well, for me being a Boss doesn't mean that you have to be in the 'corner office' of a multimillion pound business. By the same token, it doesn't mean that you're just starting out. To be honest, it captures everyone.

It also doesn't get into the debate of what makes a manager and what makes a leader... There are already plenty of books and articles you can read about that. This isn't one of them.

Instead, this book is aimed at anyone who has a team, and wants to get the best out of it, and themselves. It's for anyone who wants to find a style that works for them, that fits their own particular personality and set of values. And if for some reason your unique flavour of 'Boss' doesn't quite work for you anymore, that's fine. This is for you too.

Like anything in life, it's easy to stray from the path that suits you and your team the best. Sometimes Bosses are created out of a necessity – just to get things done. Sometimes it was more of a case of adopting the behaviours from the 'Bosses of Christmas past' and giving them a try. Behaving how you think you *should* behave as a Boss.

Then over time what might happen is the 'way it's always been done' doesn't quite feel right for you anymore, and maybe, just maybe, you start to feel as though you don't really want to be this person, this Boss, any longer. It's getting harder to achieve the results you really want... It's just not *you*! And you're right. It's not. It probably never was. It was you pretending to be something else and that can get awfully tiring after a while.

This book is about recognising that we're all different, and wonderful and unique. Just because you happen to be a Boss doesn't mean that your personality and values should be discarded and replaced by how you or others think you should behave. This book is about embracing your unique qualities and using them to their best advantage to be the Best Boss you can be – without losing yourself!

Now, before I continue I will say that this book (and this journey) isn't for everyone. After all, making the commitment to be a great Boss, an authentic Boss, isn't everyone's cup of tea. Sometimes it's just easier to do what you've always done.

After all, being different and making a change can be hard. There'll be days when it'll just be easier and quicker to do something the way you used to do it. You'll maybe slip back to how you've always worked in the past.

But the fact that you've picked up this book tells me that you're looking for something new.

Over the years, I've been fortunate enough to work with hundreds of different Bosses. Some at the very height of their career, some at the very start learning the ropes, and some in the middle. This book is a culmination of what I've learnt along the way.

In my view, the best Bosses, the ones who get the greatest results, who are happiest in their roles, are the ones working in complete alignment with themselves. With their own personality, their own values and their own strengths. Just as important are the Bosses who recognise that they're working with *people*. Real live people with ambitions, strengths, weaknesses, values and personalities all of their own.

I know this sounds super simple. Too simple maybe. But these two aspects – a happy Boss and fulfilled team members – often get lost along the way amidst day-to-day tasks, to-do lists, and just getting the job done. This scenario can, if you're not careful, lead to working just in a reactive way, a way that feels full of stress and chaos, that stifles creativity and innovation, that is focused on getting the job done at all costs, but where you're not developing or stretching yourself in any way that's useful. Instead you find yourself saying things like, 'But we've always done it like that!'

If you're sat cringing because you're already in that space, don't worry. Where you're beginning right now is exactly the right place for you.

I want you to think of this book as an annexe from all your day-to-day stuff – a mini retreat if you like – where you can escape to explore your own style, learn, grow, reflect and practise in the comfort of your own chair.

I won't drown you in theory. There are loads of books and research you can go to for that if theory is your thing. Instead, we're taking time to learn about *you* as a Boss and what you can do to get to a place where things are really working for you and your team.

To do that, we're going to be looking at your Boss Hat.

The Boss Hat is a term that's cropped up from time to time over the years. The sentence usually goes something like this... "Barbara, I'm struggling to wear the Boss Hat."

When I first heard this it made perfect sense. We've all got several hats that we wear every day. Let's use me as an easy example. As I write this the metaphorical hats that I wear are:

- *mum*
- *wife*
- *daughter*
- *sister*
- *friend*
- *coach*

- *trainer*
- *writer*
- *gardener*
- *dog walker*
- *colleague*
- *stranger on a train...*

And this list was just what popped straight into my head.

There's probably a whole load more. For each of these roles, although I remain the same person, I might be a different version of me. For example, mum, wife and friend are differing roles and I behave slightly differently for all of them, but I remain true to my own values, my own strengths, my own personality, my own sense of humour and my own reasoning.

The Boss Hat is the same. It's just another hat in a long list of hats that you already own, and take on and off seamlessly throughout your day. It may demand another side of you to come forward, but you're still the same person wearing the hat.

Let's take a look at what this means for your journey as a Boss.

STEP 1 – DESIGNING YOUR HAT

In order to wear your Boss Hat with pride, you first need to ensure it fits your head perfectly. In this step, we're going to be taking a good look at what matters to you and how you can use your values to be a great Boss.

STEP 2 – LOOKING AFTER YOUR HAT

As with most situations in life, you can't look after anything else properly unless you're taking care of yourself. This step is all about how to do that without taking your eye off the ball.

STEP 3 – WEARING YOUR HAT

In this step, you'll explore 10 habits to weave into your day that will help you wear your hat with pride and feel comfortable doing so.

STEP 4 – PASSING ON THE HAT

A great Boss understands when they need to pass on their hat to someone else. This doesn't mean giving up, but more sharing the load.

Throughout each step you'll find exercises to complete. Each is designed to get you thinking, exploring and reflecting.

To get you underway, here are some tips that might just come in handy as you progress through this book.

- Don't aim to read this book from cover to cover without stopping. Yes, do start at the front, but when you get to an exercise or activity, pause and work your way through it before continuing.

- Make some time each day to at least do one of the sections. Find a quiet spot. Grab a cup of tea, coffee, or whatever your tipple is, and get started. It might help to have a notebook to hand so you can scribble your thoughts down as you go.

- Remember to get your free resources over at: **www.barbaranixon.co.uk/bosshatfreebonuses** I'll give you a nudge throughout the book if there's something you need to download.

Everything else I'll leave up to you...

As I mentioned, this book is like a mental retreat just for you. An opportunity for you to examine where you are now, how you want to develop and change. No pressure, no fuss, just you finding the right Boss Hat to fit.

Enjoy!

Barbara

"

It doesn't matter who you used to be, what matters is who you are today.

"

– Unknown

STEP 1: DESIGNING YOUR HAT

Over the years, I've always been the type of person to get a kick out of jumping in feet first. The problem with this strategy is that even though you learn loads (and learn fast), more often than not you have to back track at some point and build some strong foundations.

Your Boss Hat is no different.

In the time that you've been leading a team, you will have learnt so much already. What has worked, what hasn't, what really really hasn't! What you're going to keep doing, what you never ever want to do again. And although all of this learning is worth its weight in gold, it can sometimes feel as though that's all you're doing – trying and testing new skills and techniques as you go along. It becomes exhausting and you may find yourself thinking *there has to be an easier way*.

Maybe this is something you can relate to?

And there is an easier way. But it involves doing some ground work first and allowing yourself some time to build strong foundations that will hold you steady in good times and bad. That's what Designing Your Hat is all about – understanding yourself better.

By tapping into what motivates you, what makes you tick, what you enjoy, what your pet hates are, what you value, and what calms you down, you'll not only be able to structure your day and develop a routine with useful habits, but you'll also feel so much more in tune with what matters to you and where to focus your energy. As a result, you'll probably find decision-making much easier. You'll also feel much more confident as you go about your day.

BY KNOWING YOURSELF, YOU'LL START TO KNOW OTHERS BETTER.

So many Bosses don't take the time or opportunity to do this essential ground work – instead they jump straight into focusing on how they can 'manage their team'. But by thoroughly understanding what's important to you, it'll take away some of the guess work in your interactions and routines. And then, you'll start to 'feel it'.

Ready to learn what matters to you? Let's dive in and design your Boss Hat.

" Life isn't about finding yourself, it's about creating yourself. "

— George Bernard Shaw

WHAT DOES BEING A GREAT BOSS MEAN TO YOU?

Let me ask you a question. When I say the word 'Boss', what springs to mind?

Over the years, I've asked variations of this question to the people I've worked with and now it's your turn...

By taking time to get underneath what the word 'Boss' means to you, and more to the point what being a *great* Boss means to you, you'll start to zone in on what you deem important.

But here's the catch... Over the years, you may have had numerous Bosses. From your very first job, to the last person you ever worked for. You may also have had different types of Bosses, from those that you'd definitely work for again any day of the week, to those that you'd cross the street to avoid today.

It's fair to say that Bosses come in all shapes and sizes, but there's only one *you*, so it's important right now to focus on what being a great Boss signifies in your own mind without being influenced by anything else.

l you why this is important.

In order for you to develop, learn and grow, you need to figure out where you're heading. It's just like getting into a car: without knowing where you're going, you might have a lovely joy ride, but you're probably not going to get anywhere specific. By having a good think about what your definition of a great Boss is, you can use this to build on as you go through the book. And you'll have a much better idea of the direction you wish to take.

So, your very first task is to clear your mind and scribble down your thoughts.

- What does being a great Boss mean to you?
- What does a great Boss do?

Now that you've downloaded your definition of being a great Boss, glance down at your list and imagine yourself two to three years from now. Let's pretend that you're receiving an award for your leadership skills within your organisation. (If you struggle to visualise things like this, just go with me on this one. No-one needs to know.)

Picture this... The awards are taking place at a prestigious hotel. It's a black tie event and everyone (let's say around 200-300 people) is looking glamorous sat around their tables drinking their glasses of fizz. Standing at the podium on the stage is someone you admire greatly. They're introducing you by telling everyone how wonderful you are and why you're receiving this award.

Now, take a moment and write down what they say about you. (Just a note here. It doesn't have to be perfect. No-one's going to look at it so feel free to go to town.) Be as descriptive as you can. Remember it's in the future so try to move past feeling as though this would never happen, or you don't know what to say. The key here is to write down how you'd love to be described, using words that are meaningful to you.

Here's an example to give you an idea:

Over the three years that Jean has been leading 'Boss Inc', the company has gone from strength to strength. What started as an idea in her kitchen quickly grew into a brand we all know and love today, and the reason for this is clear. Jean's authentic and unique leadership has steered the ship through good times and bad. She has a real knack for communicating effectively to her team, and listening to what really matters and will make a difference to the business, always recognising that her team really is the heart and soul of the business.

As well has her undeniable leadership qualities, Jean prides herself on being visible, approachable and available for everyone in her organisation no matter what role they play.

Now it's your turn.

If you're struggling have a think about the answers to these questions:

- What you want to be known for?
- What do you want others to think of you?
- How do you want to behave?

- What have you achieved so far?
- How would you want others to describe your personality?
- What matters to you?

Take a minute to re-read it. Feels good to have a vision, doesn't it?!

I know that this scenario might seem a bit far-fetched or pie-in-the-sky, but that doesn't matter. What matters here is that you've taken the time to write down what's important, what you're shooting for, how you want to be perceived, how you want to behave. All of this is crucial for creating your Boss Hat because it lays a foundation for where you're heading.

Now before we go on, grab a highlighter or your pen and go back over the speech that you wrote. Highlight the key words for you. The words that speak to you most.

For example if 'Jean' was doing this exercise it might look like this:

Over the three years that Jean has been leading 'Boss Inc', the company has gone from strength to strength. What started as an idea in her kitchen quickly grew into a brand we all know and love today, and the reason for this is clear. Jean's authentic and unique leadership has steered the ship through good times and bad. She has a real knack for ***communicating*** *effectively to her team, and* ***listening*** *to what really matters and will make a difference to the business always recognising that her team really are the heart and soul of the business.*

As well has her undeniable leadership qualities, Jean prides herself on being ***visible***, ***approachable*** *and* ***available*** *for everyone in her organisation no matter what role they play.*

You may have words like:

honest, reliable, patient, enthusiastic, generous, outgoing, calm, confident, fun, approachable, understanding, caring, ambitious, tenacious, assertive, passionate, hard-working, considerate, loyal, loving, determined, supportive etc.

Once you've captured your key words from your speech, put them into an order of importance. Keep shuffling them around until you're happy with your order. When you've done that, whittle them down to the top three most important words and make sure that you're happy with the three you've chosen.

Three Values

1.

2.

3.

These are the values that matter to you. These are the traits that are your guiding light. When you're wondering what decision to make, when you're wondering what the right answer is, when you're wondering whether you should do something or not... *these* are the words that will guide you to your answer. The answer that's most *you*.

You know that gut feeling you get in the pit of your stomach when you're about to do something? The one that tells you whether you're doing something right or wrong? That's your values talking to you. Learning what they are and what they mean to you will help you focus on the right course of action whenever you're up against the wall. They're also great to communicate to your team so they know exactly what's important to you.

The next step is to glance over the speech once again and take a look at areas you need to develop.

We all have areas where we need to learn, practise and develop. This book will throw up all kinds of points to work on as you go along. For now, take a look at the speech you wrote about yourself and see if anything pops out at you. For example, you might have written that you're a great communicator and listener but you know that you've got some work to do in this area. You may have written that you're great at delegating and developing your team but deep down you know that you need to take a look at this... And it's okay to need to improve some parts of yourself. As I said, the speech was written for a future you, so there's time to get everything in place. We'll be covering skills later on in the book too, so no rush. For now, pop on over to **www.barbaranixon.co.uk/bosshatfreebonuses** and download your development plan where you can capture your values and growth areas.

WHAT'S YOUR STORY?

When you start to think about where you're heading and what you want to improve, it's easy to forget where you've been and all the amazing stuff you've already done to get you to where you are now.

This is especially tricky when you're used to getting something done and moving straight on to the next task, or project. Often we forget to take the time to celebrate our successes, or even to reflect on how far we've come, but we must. Because *that* is our story. Yes, we've all got one, and it's something that many people dismiss, disregard and often take for granted. But sharing your story is oh-so-very important.

Now, you might be thinking *but my story is really not that interesting*. But it really is! Because it's what makes you you. And when people are getting to know you, they need (and want) to know what you've done up until this point.

Let me explain. When we meet people, our brains are looking for aspects of them that we have in common. Did you grow up in the same neighbourhood? Go to the same school? Work in the same company? Support the same team? Know the same people? Like the same restaurants, books, movies?

How many times have you had conversations where you suddenly feel an affinity with the other person, for no other reason than you have something in common?

Yes, there is a risk that you might not have anything in common with your team, but by sharing your story you're giving others the opportunity to find something about you that they can relate to, empathise with, respect, be inspired by, be motivated by, laugh about, or find interesting.

Now, you might also be thinking that your story is no-one else's business and that letting other people 'in' will actually take away some of your credibility. But here's the thing... When you're leading a team, it's important that your team trusts you. After all you can't and won't follow someone you don't trust.

Team members might do as they're told because their Boss asked them to do something, but they'll always find themselves on the lookout for the hidden agenda. That might start to affect your role as the Boss, as well as your working relationship with your team. Also, your team are much more likely to work together and support each other if they trust each other too.

That trust starts with you.

Your team knows you're not a robot that lives at the office. They realise you have a life outside of work. Having a story is not going to come as a massive shock to them. After all, we've all started somewhere, and you're no different.

You might also be wondering *but what if they think I'm a fake and that I don't know anything?* especially if this is your first time leading a team. We'll come to that in more detail shortly, but for now just know that we've all felt like that at some point or another. This is a natural emotion that you're experiencing, but don't let that stop you from sharing your story.

Sharing your story is a great way to build trust, but this doesn't just happen overnight. It takes time. If you think of a relationship you have with someone you trust, chances are that trust didn't just appear as soon as you met each other. It was built up over time as you got to know them. The trust in your relationships with your team is no different. The more they learn about you and your journey, the more likely they are to trust you.

As we learn about others, our brains are also looking out for the parts of them that resonate with us. That's what your team members are doing. The mistakes you've made, the people you've met, what you find funny, how you bounce back after failure, and how you got to where you are today. They're looking for signs that you're just like them. That you're human. That you understand each other. And all of this helps you build a foundation perfect for trust to form.

As well as building trust there's also another bonus to sharing your story. It's a great reminder of where you've come from, but more importantly just how far you've come. Be proud of it.

So, let's give this a try. Spend a few moments having a think back over your journey and write it down.

You might find answering these questions helpful:

- How did you get to where you are now?
- What was your first job?
- What did it teach you?
- Why did you decide to take this job/work at this company?
- What do you enjoy most about your job?

- What's your biggest success?
- What's your funniest anecdote?
- What's your biggest failure or mistake?
- Who gave you your first big break?
- Where are you heading?
- What's your vision?
- What do you do outside of work?
- Do you have a family?
- What hobbies do you have?
- What's important to you?
- What are your pet hates?
- What do you want for the team/department/company?

As you're going through your story, you might start to remember little anecdotes that serve as mini stories about different topics. Make a note of these as you go a long too.

Now that you've had a think about your story, remember this isn't a one-way street where you just start talking at your team telling them everything about yourself. Your story is for you to have up your sleeve as you're getting to know your team so they can get to know you in conversation. You'll have your funny stories on the tip of your tongue when you need them and you'll know exactly what story to use as you're chatting to the team so they get to know you.

As I mentioned, trust doesn't just happen. It takes a while to build up... But just seconds to destroy. So, while you're working hard to build a trusting relationship, you also need to think about how you're going to keep it. We'll come back to that later in the book.

WHAT GETS YOU OUT OF BED?

Whether we realise it or not, we all have a 'why' – a reason for doing what we're doing, our main motivator, the something that drives us when things get tough and what keeps us moving forwards. It's this 'why' that is unique to you and often linked to an emotion. And even though your 'why' might have been doing its job behind the scenes, it's worth knowing and bringing to the forefront, because it can be a powerful motivator when things are not quite going to plan, or when you lose sight of where you're heading. For example, you may be desperate to be a great Boss to someone because you had a particularly great Boss who believed in you earlier in your career, so now you want to do the same for someone else.

It may be that you want to feel aligned in your role so that people can see the real you and you'll feel happier at work.

It may be that you had a particularly bad experience with a Boss and you want to be different for other people.

It might be that you want your company to be a fun and fulfilling place to work, and for people to love being there.

By taking the time to drill down into your 'why', you'll have the strongest motivator right at your fingertips when you need it most.

We all have those days when we just can't be bothered. Where nothing seems to be going our way and we don't know why we even started this in the first place. Those days when you find yourself thinking *I tried, but it didn't work so I'm not going to bother anymore*. Yep, we've all been there.

But this is just what growth is like. The best way I can describe it is if you were training for a big event. A while back I was training to do the Oxfam Trailtrekker. This is a 100k walk in 30 hours. Now, I couldn't have just turned up and gone *ta-da, let's walk 100k today!* I'd never have achieved anything. It was too big a leap. So I broke it down into small chunks and started training.

This sounds easier than it was in reality. There were days when the weather was rubbish, it was cold, windy and rainy, and I didn't want to leave the house to go for a long walk. Then there were days when my muscles ached and I felt like giving up. To be honest, if I hadn't taken the time to zone in on my 'why' – the reason I was doing it in the first place – quitting would've probably been inevitable.

Instead, whenever I felt like I'd hit the wall I reminded myself of my 'why' and just kept training.

Your 'why' will do just the same. It'll be your north star on those days when everything seems to be going wrong, when you're tired, stressed and fed up. On days like these, this is where your why comes into its own.

So, let's have a go at writing it.

Before you get cracking, I'll give you some tips to make this easier and more powerful for you.

If I asked you why you're doing what you're doing, the quickest and most obvious answer might be 'money'. And that's fine. But rather than just focusing on money – which believe it or not isn't always a massive motivator – think of what money gives you. This might be security; to allow you to look after your family; to give you the ability to travel; to pursue a hobby that you're passionate about. Get the idea?

Don't be afraid to dig a bit deeper to get into your core why. Give yourself the time to think.

Write your why here, and when you're done, make a note of it somewhere you can easily find it when you need to refer to it.

DESIGNING YOUR HAT: A RECAP

In this section, we've talked about how designing your Boss Hat means finding out about you. What makes you tick? What's important to you? What's brought you to where you are today?

All of this will give you a solid foundation on which to build your future as a Boss.

If you haven't already, make sure you have a go at these exercises before you move on:

- What does being a great Boss mean to you?
- What are your values?
- What's your story?
- Write your why

And don't forget to download the additional resources at **www.barbaranixon.co.uk/bosshatfreebonuses**

Now that you've Designed Your Hat, we're going to be exploring how to look after it properly.

"

To be really of use to others, means you must first take care of yourself completely and fully.

"

STEP 2: LOOKING AFTER YOUR HAT

Throughout my career, the one thing I've discovered that I absolutely know to be true is that being a Boss isn't just about taking care of business. It isn't just about the day-to-day tasks. It also isn't just about taking care of the people, even though, yes, all of those things are important. It isn't *predominantly* about either of these, even though you might be thinking otherwise (and pushing yourself every day to make sure these bases are covered).

No, there is a missing piece to the puzzle that needs to be managed, very carefully, because if you don't take care of it, it could cause everything else to crumble into nothing... And that's *you*!

BEING A BOSS IS A TOUGH JOB THAT REQUIRES YOU TO ABSOLUTELY TAKE CARE OF YOURSELF.

Now, before you skip over this chapter with a 'yeah, yeah, I know I need to eat, sleep and exercise!' I'm talking a bit more than that. This chapter is about knowing yourself better than ever before and putting in the strategies that you need to ensure you're always working at the top of your game. I mean, let's face it, how can you expect to give your all to your team and your work when you're not looking after yourself properly?

Think of it this way... You know when you're on a plane and you're listening to the safety announcement which says something like, 'Put on your own oxygen mask first before you see to anyone else?' This is exactly the same. You can't be of service to anyone else if you're feeling stressed, overwhelmed, under pressure, or out of control.

So, before we continue, I'm giving you permission throughout this section of the book to be completely selfish and just think about you. If this makes you feel a bit uncomfortable just go with it for a while, because this stuff really matters. In this step, we're going to go a bit deeper into what I've noticed are the common road blocks for successful Bosses. You'll create strategies to help you side step those road blocks when they arise.

This is all about creating good habits that will serve you for the long term, to make sure you're well looked after, because if you don't put some great habits in place here, you might find yourself further down the line wishing you had.

So, before we start, let's do a bit of a sense check with where you are right now.

Take a couple of minutes to think through your average day and week. Rate yourself for where you are right now. Before you start, let me give you a couple of rules. Firstly, there's no wrong answer. No-one's checking up on you, so be honest with yourself. Secondly, think about how you feel. What's your body telling you? Is there room for improvement?

For this exercise, use T = TRUE or F = FALSE.

THE LOOKING AFTER YOUR HAT SENSE CHECK QUIZ

1. I am more reactive than proactive.
2. I sometimes find myself doubting my ability.
3. There are times when I feel fraudulent and wonder how I got to where I am.
4. I find myself thinking about work when I'm at home.
5. I find myself checking my phone/emails out of hours.
6. I struggle to switch off and relax in the evening and sometimes wake up in the middle of the night.
7. I don't make time for hobbies or the things I enjoy.
8. I feel rushed through the day and a slave to my 'to do' list.

9. I'm surrounded by people who bring me down and are negative.

10. I find myself questioning my decisions and wondering whether I'm good enough.

11. I find myself struggling to switch off on holiday and often continue to check my e-mails

12. I find myself reaching for my phone as soon as I wake up

13. I feel lacking in confidence sometimes

14. I feel my work life balance is out of kilter

15. I feel as though I have to do everything myself

Everywhere you've put a T, make a note of it in your development plan as something you need to work on. But don't worry too much about it yet. Self-awareness is the best first step for change.

Let's delve a bit deeper, shall we?

WHAT ARE YOUR RULES?

As we go about our day-to-day lives, there are some things that help us perform at our best. And then there are things that do anything but. We all have them, and the sooner we figure out what our own personal rules are, the better.

Let me explain.

Our own personal rules are what we absolutely *need* to be able to be on our A game, the invisible lines that we just won't cross.

For example, for some it might be a tidy and organised desk; leaving bang on 5pm so they can pick up their child and enjoy their evening; arriving extra early into work so they can get all of their focus work done before everyone else gets in; a walk at lunch time; or a meeting-free day once a week, never taking work home, or always having some time on a Friday to reflect and plan. This list isn't exhaustive and can be a million different things for each of us.

By taking the time to identify what the rules are for ourselves, we are putting in some boundaries to our working day, so that we get the most out of our time and make progress in a way that is good for us without causing us to feel overwhelmed, stressed, burnt-out, or running on a hamster wheel.

Now, although we may have rules floating around that help us and we may even adhere to them from time to time, quite often our boundaries are invisible to others and go un-noticed. We might even have amazing days when everything comes together and where we find ourselves thinking *why don't I always do that because that works well for me?*

If that thought pops into your mind, you've hit on the very rule you're looking for.

Some might spring to mind instantly. Using myself as an example for a minute, I work best when I've had some time outside first. So, I go for a walk before I start work. There are days when I look outside and it's pouring down with rain and I don't bother. And of course, those are the days I just don't get my best work done.

Now the secret here is to try not to be influenced by what you think you *should* be doing, or what you've just got into the habit of doing. For example, at the minute, you may get to work and as soon as you've got your morning coffee you sit at your computer and check your emails. Now, secretly you know that this is just a habit and that you don't actually have to check your email first thing. In fact, you know your day goes better if you do something else first like going round and saying good morning to your team, or getting stuck into a particular project.

Yes, there may be tasks that you absolutely have to do during your day as part of your role, and that's fine. We all have those and your rules aren't about only doing what you enjoy or keeping a rule at the expense of other work that needs doing. Your rules should work around the procedures in your organisation. For example, if you have to work weekends to keep up with your customers orders and your rule is to have the weekends off, then chances are it isn't going to happen. Ultimately, we need to be realistic. However, identifying what your rules are and how you can make them work for you is a great way to make you conscious about how you personally work at your best.

But what if you can't quite put your finger on what those rules are for you?

Recently, I took my kids to the dentist. My youngest was 8 and my son was 16 at the time. The dentist spoke to them about how to brush properly and she said something that stuck with me. She said, 'For a couple of minutes while you're brushing, focus only on brushing. It's easy to get distracted and think about other things, but for a couple of minutes consciously think about brushing your teeth, on what you're doing, and how you're doing the best job you can.'

Hmmm... mindful brushing!

Now, this struck me because it's true of so much that we do in the day, isn't it? As we go about our day, so much of it is done in autopilot. We adopt habits and they control us, instead of us being in control of our day. Whether these are good or bad habits doesn't matter. Then there are days when, as I mentioned, everything works perfectly. We feel so much better, in control, calm and in the zone. Yet it's tricky to pinpoint what we've done differently, so it becomes hard to repeat. More to the point, we give ourselves an excuse for not being able to repeat it.

'If only every day could be like this...'

But what if we went through our day 'consciously brushing' to see what was working for us and what wasn't? What would that be like?

So, let's give it a try.

This is our next exercise and it's split into two parts. The first part involves you sitting down and reflecting on what you need in order to be on your A-game.

- Do you need to get into work early?
- Do you need an immaculate desk?
- Do you need to get outside at lunch?
- Do you need to spend some time talking to your team?
- Do you need to be able to leave at a certain time?

Have a think about what this is for you.

The second part is to go about your work as you normally would, but this time try to consciously think about what you're doing that works for you, and what doesn't (but has become a habit anyway).

To do this, you'll have to work on being mindful and in the present moment. As you go about your day, make a note of the helpful behaviours and practices that you notice.

What are you doing differently?

What has to happen on a regular basis in order for the magic to continue to happen?

What should your daily rules be for you to always be at your best?

Make a note of these.

Once you've got them, put them in order of importance from 1 to 10 and focus on making the top three into a habit.

1.

2.

3.

4.

5.

6.

7.

8.

9.

10.

They're important to you. They make your day better, so consistently and consciously weave them into your working hours.

BANISHING YOUR DEMONS

It doesn't matter where we are on our career ladder or in our lives; the one thing we can be sure of is that at some point along the way we'll have to banish some demons. You know, those limiting beliefs that pop up in your head to tell you that you're not good enough.

Over the years, I've called these Managers' Demons, but to be entirely honest they aren't specific to managers in particular. In fact, I'm willing to bet that we've all had them at one time or another.

In case you're wondering, a demon is that little creature that sits on your shoulder (or the voice in the back of your head) that tells you you're not good enough; that other people are doing better; that people prefer someone else to you; that you shouldn't even try because you're going to fail; that you're going to be 'found out' any second because how you got to where you are today is a complete and utter fluke.

Any of this sound familiar?

That inner doubt that you get when you need to be at your

best, when you need to make an important phone call, do a big presentation, make a decision, make a pitch or step out of your comfort zone in some way.

These are all our demons coming out to play. If you're reading this thinking *yes that's me*, let me assure you that you're not alone. We've all been there, and will probably continue to go there as we grow, develop and evolve, but even so they can certainly feel disconcerting. You might be going along fine doing your thing and then these pesky demons come along and catch you off guard, which can knock your confidence. It takes a while to get back into your stride after that, doesn't it, as you try to motivate yourself once again?

But I absolutely 100% know that owning a demon (or a few of them) is not a sign of weakness. In fact, it's exactly the opposite. It's a sign that you're stepping out of your comfort zone and growing. By facing up to your demons and seeing them for what they are, you can start to do something about them.

So, let's do that now, shall we?

Take a moment to have a think and then write down what your demons are.

Just to give you a bit of a hand, common ones I've come across are:

- I'm not good enough.
- I don't really know what I'm doing.
- Other people are better than me.
- I'm scared of making a mistake.
- What will others think?

Well done. Identifying them is a great start. As I've already mentioned, demons are perfectly normal and very common.

So, with that in mind, I want to give you permission to just realise that even though your demons raise their heads every now and again, you do still achieve an awful lot in your day. So go easy on yourself! Recognise that you're doing a great job. Just by being aware of where you are right now is a fantastic first step.

So, now that you've identified these demons, have a think about when they tend to come out to play. Is there something particular that you do that kickstarts these feelings? Do they tend to happen when you're doing a particular task? Or at a certain time of day?

"I have written eleven books, but each time I think, 'Uh, oh, they're going to find out now. I've run a game on everybody, and they're going to find me out."

– Maya Angelou

Although these demons can be tough to shrug off sometimes the best way to banish them is to accept that they're a natural result of you growing and changing. For example, when you start to exercise, your muscles hurt as you push yourself and get stronger and fitter. It doesn't mean there's anything wrong, as such, but just that you're moving forward. Your demons are similar. In my experience, they tend to come out to play when you're stretching and pushing through your comfort zone. Although it's good to take note of your feelings, your demons aren't there to dictate what you should do next, nor where you should go. That's your job. You're in the driving seat, not them.

You've identified your demons and when they tend to rear their heads. You know that you're not alone and that it's just your comfort zone stretching. Let's take a look at how you can get better at banishing your demons.

WHAT DO YOU BRING TO THE PARTY?

One of the most common demons that I've come across is not feeling good enough and thinking that we don't have the right skills at all. The problem with this belief is it's not true. Usually, we are more than good enough, but we don't take the time to think about what we have done. Instead, we finish one project and move straight onto the next one without stopping to reflect or celebrate, so let's take a look at what you're great at by having a think about what skills you bring to your role.

Write a list of 10 skills that you bring to your role. Remember to stay positive.

My Skills

1.

2.

3.

4.

5.

6.

7.

8.

9.

10.

Once we've been doing something for a while, it's easy to forget why and how we got there, but this is worth remembering as it's what other people see in you. These are the positives. You got to where you are today for a reason. It didn't just happen overnight. You worked at it. Where you are today is a result of your blood, sweat and tears and you've probably got the bruises to prove it. Just like your story, the skills you've gained along the way shouldn't be ignored; they should be celebrated. Remind yourself of this, whenever you need to.

Now, the next step is to come up with three achievements you've made since being in your role. I'm absolutely positive that you've achieved more than three, but these are the achievements you're most proud of reaching. Again, don't think too much about it; just have a go at writing down what comes into your head first.

Remembering the great moments where we've seen success is good for us. These are proud moments, so try to look down the list and truly feel that pride and success in yourself. If you find yourself thinking they were a stroke of luck because someone gave you a hand, stop! Think of them as achievements that you can hang your hat on. Have belief in your own abilities and trust what you can do.

Now that you've set the ball rolling, one great idea to keep the momentum is to keep a celebration diary. This is a journal where you keep a note of what has gone well, no matter how big or small the success. It can be as simple as 'had time to grab a coffee from my favourite coffee shop before work' to 'launched my big project' and everything in between.

This will not only work to help banish your demons as you'll be focusing your mind on the positives of what you've done and reflecting on them when you need a pick-me-up, but it's a moment to pause if you're the type of person who goes straight from one task or project to another without taking the time to stop and congratulate yourself. If that's you, this'll help you to take a moment before rushing into the next task and make sure you digest all the good work you've done.

Keeping track of your celebrations is a task that will mean developing a habit, especially if you've not kept a journal before. So here's a couple of points to remember. You don't have to write long passages each day. I keep a celebration journal and some days it's just bullet points, whereas other days I feel the need to write a couple of pages. Whatever you feel like doing is perfectly fine. There's no pressure at all.

You're also not just looking for those major achievements to celebrate, for instance, finishing a five-year project or getting a promotion. The small things are just as important. So today, I might celebrate catching up with an old friend, finishing this section of writing *The Boss Hat* and going out for dinner with my husband. You don't have to celebrate just the big stuff. All we're doing is re-training our brain to recognise and celebrate the small stuff that makes up our lives.

Obviously, the big stuff would feature too but we don't go about life with something huge happening every single day. If we were to wait for the massive milestones then we'd have nothing to put in our journal. If you're working towards something major, make sure you're celebrating those milestones as well. The small goals that you need to achieve to get you closer to completing the end goal.

The best way to go about doing this is to decide what the best time would be for you to spend five minutes celebrating your day. It might be on the train home, as you close down your PC before you leave, taking a break in the afternoon... The choice is yours. Then set an alarm on your phone so you remember. Then set five minutes on your timer (again on your phone) and focus for that time on writing down bullets of everything that's gone well. You don't need a special notepad unless you want one. You can also find a template in the book resources section here.

No over-thinking, no overwhelm, no frills, no fuss!

Done.

To get you started, have a go at journaling here.

Day 1

Day 2

Day 3

Day 4

Day 5

COMPARISON PARALYSIS

It's so easy these days with social media and the internet to fall down the rabbit hole of comparing yourself to other people, from your old school friends on Facebook, to your colleagues and peers on LinkedIn. Before long, you're sat in a heap of self-pity thinking that everyone is doing better than you.

But by comparing yourself, you're not actually being fair to them or to yourself. As my mum used to say, "You never know what's going on behind closed doors". For all you know they could be looking at you and thinking the exact same thing.

By all means look around and learn from other people. If they're great at something learn from them, but don't try to emulate them or compare yourself to them by putting them on a pedestal and belittling yourself. That is a road to nowhere!

By the same token, worrying what other people think of you is not helpful.

"A day of worry is more exhausting than a week of work."

- John Lubbock

It is so easy to get caught up with wondering what other people will think that we forget to think about what we want to do or what is the right direction to take.

Give yourself a break from analysing the thoughts of others and remember that this journey is all about you creating your own Boss Hat, not about wearing someone else's. There is only one *you* in the world and only one way of you being a Boss that fits your personality, your values and your strengths.

So, when you find yourself in comparison paralysis just smile, wish them well and crack on with your own journey.

WORK YOUR WEB

How often do you consciously work your network?

Finding the time to nurture your network is a great habit to get into for many reasons, but when you're busy doing the day-to-day activities, it can be first to slip from your to-do list. Nurturing and consciously building a wider, stronger network, though, will *always* be a beneficial use of your time.

Being well connected allows you to learn from other people; to see what's best practice outside the confines of your company; and to meet new people with a different perspective. Strong networks will also be there to recommend people who can lend a hand when you need it; to introduce you to other good contacts; to help with problem-solving; or to act as a pool of resource when you're recruiting. Networks will do all of that and more, and will set you apart from your peers instantly, if you take the time to nurture it.

So, this is the clincher. We're not just talking about numbers here. So many people think that a strong network is just collecting contacts on somewhere like LinkedIn, or having a pile of business cards in your drawer. You have to go a bit deeper.

We're talking about building relationships with people. Getting to know them and allowing them to get to know you. Just like everything we've already spoken about in the previous step Designing Your Hat, a strong network is all about people who know who you are so that you're the one that they think about and trust when it matters most.

In order to do this, you don't have to attend networking events that you don't enjoy. It doesn't mean standing around in a room with lots of other people juggling your cup of tea and business cards. It can just be as simple as reaching out to external contacts you already have and arranging to meet and chat over a coffee. You could also look into any institutes that are connected with your industry in your local area and attend one of their events. Often these are great for your personal development as well. Lots of industries have their own institutes that you can attend if you became a member (or quite often as a guest at least once). During these events, not only will you meet like-minded people in your industry, but more often than not they'll have a speaker presenting on their specialist topic, which will also develop your knowledge and keep you ahead of any best practice that's relevant to you.

If you're wondering where to start, here are some pointers for you:

- Ask some of your peers which networking events they attend and make a list here.

- Research some industry-specific events in your local area and make contact with the organiser or go along as a guest.

- Reach out to some of your network to ask for a catch up over a coffee.

FIND YOUR CHEERLEADERS

As you're thinking about your network, you'll probably start to be more aware of the attitude of the people you're hanging around. It's so easy to find yourself surrounded by negative people, or as I call them Subtractors. People who seem to suck all the life force out of you like JK Rowling's Dementors. They sap you of your energy and anything positive you were feeling. Want an example? They're the people who will tell you it'll rain tomorrow when you're enjoying a lovely sunny day. You know that type of person, right?

"If you hang out with chickens, you're going to cluck and if you hang out with eagles, you're going to fly."

- Steve Maraboli

We've all got people like that in our lives. It might even be that you're related to them. And that's okay. It doesn't mean that you have to remove them completely from your life (especially if you're married to one!) but what you can do is work on building a tribe of your very own cheerleaders. These are the people who make you feel energised rather than drained; propel you forwards; are naturally positive in their attitude; want to see you (and everyone for that matter) succeed; are constantly on the lookout for how we can achieve an outcome and get things done; and are great at tackling obstacles and solving problems. They're the people who simply radiate positive energy in all directions. These are the people you need in your corner.

Right now you might be thinking *but where do I find these people?*

Well, look no further. The beauty of this is they're everywhere. It might be in a group on Facebook or LinkedIn. It might be a networking group that you go to. It might be a sports team, or a group connected to a hobby. These people are absolutely everywhere. You just need to make a conscious decision to seek them out and look for them. Have you ever noticed that when you decide to buy a new car you suddenly see the same car everywhere? The same goes for finding your cheerleaders. Once you've made up your mind to start seeking out like-minded positive people, you'll start spotting them everywhere.

You might also find that as you become a cheerleader for others, you'll naturally attract like-minded people who want to spend time with you.

So, this exercise is a fun one. Spend the next 48 hours just being on the lookout for positive cheerleaders and see who you can find.

My Cheerleaders

GRAB SOME ME-TIME

As you're looking after your hat, one of the best and easiest ways to do this is to get some time to yourself.

As I write this, I can hear you laughing from here...

"Are you kidding, Barbara? I barely have enough time to eat, let alone have some time to myself!"

If this is you, listen up as this is important.

Running at full pelt all the time just isn't healthy. Yes, it might feel great at the start. (As someone who used to leave all my assignments to the last minute when I was a student just so I could feel great working under pressure, I know what this feels like.) Doing that day in, day out, though, can really start to wear you down. You wouldn't let your car run on empty as after a while it would just stop right there wherever it was. You're no different. Working non-stop is no doubt doing you a lot more harm than good in the long run.

The other side of the coin is that it's probably impacting your team as you role model long working hours every day. It doesn't matter how often you tell people to go home or that they don't have to work long hours just because you do. Whether you like it or not, or realise it or not, this behaviour is drip-feeding into their subconscious as something they should be doing as well. Before you know it, you'll have a team working into the night every night and feeling run down and resentful. So, if you're not willing to change this habit for yourself, time to do it for your team, because having a team of stressed and tired people isn't a great place to be.

In the long run, it's also impacting on the way that you think as you're not giving your brain any respite at all. Your brain needs rest as much as anything.

Here in the 21st century, we're bombarding our brains 24/7. There literally is no let up from the information overload that we're experiencing. Unless we allow our brains time to stop and rest up once in a while, it'll start to affect the way that we think, our concentration levels, and potentially our decision-making and problem-solving ability.

I once heard a story about a couple of lumberjacks who were competing to see who could cut down the most trees. The first lumberjack worked tirelessly cutting trees down one after another, not stopping for a second. Every so often he could hear the other lumberjack stop for a moment and this would just spur him on knowing that he would surely be in the lead as he hadn't stopped once. When it came to the end and the results were being read out, the first lumberjack was shocked to hear that he hadn't actually come first.

"How did that happen? Surely there's been a mistake. I kept hearing you stop."

To which the second lumberjack replied, "That was when I was sharpening my axe."

Taking the time to sharpen your axe is crucial for everyone. By doing so, you'll find that your brain works more effectively, having had some downtime. Have you ever noticed that your best aha moments or ideas come when you're doing something mundane like having a shower, driving your car, brushing your teeth or walking the dog? This is because you've stepped away from all the daily craziness, giving your brain a well-deserved rest and the perfect chance to do a bit of brain admin.

There are all sorts of ways that you can do this. The first way is to give yourself permission to have some downtime. It doesn't have to be all day. Even 30 minutes a day will do you the world of good.

Next, have a think about what you enjoy doing. It might be going for a walk, reading a book, something creative like painting or drawing, riding your bike, building a model, singing in a choir, or maybe some gardening. Activities that give your brain the chance to either be completely focused in whatever you're doing (cooking, reading, painting) or allow your brain to just wander (taking a walk, swimming, riding a bike). Whatever it is, dedicate some time each day even if it's just for a short amount of time.

Make a list here of a maximum of three things that you enjoy doing that would help you to relax and switch off. Plot some time in your diary for when you're going to do them.

As well as giving your brain a break, booking a meeting with yourself once a week is a great way to give you time to reflect and plan for the future. You might find that as you're 'in' the daily work load, getting the opportunity to think and plan is near to impossible. If this is you, have a go at booking in a meeting with yourself each week. If you have an accessible online calendar where other people can book in time with you, lock in time for yourself so that you know this slot can't be snatched up. Then you're able to use it to plan for the following week or month, or get some much-needed focus time on a project.

LET'S GET ORGANISED

As well as looking after yourself, looking after your hat also means having everything you need in place to ensure you feel completely in control. That's where good systems and processes come in. Without them, you may find yourself easily stressed and overwhelmed, like you're just chasing your tail. And let's be honest, great systems can also save you a tonne of time.

But before we talk about the systems that you've currently got in place, or that you need to get, let's get *completely* organised from top to bottom.

I know, I can hear you groaning from here. And yes, you might be thinking that you haven't got the time to do this right now. Be honest... you haven't got the time not to, right? This is short-term pain for a lifetime of gain, so set aside an hour a week for the next few weeks and take it one step at a time.

Things to focus on:

- Sorting out your drawers
- Going through your desk

- Going through your filing cabinets
- Creating folders that will work for you

All of this might seem like a pain, but time spent searching for stuff is time you could be doing things that matter. Being organised will also help your team to be more organised as well, because you'll be setting up processes that work.

Once you've organised your working environment, it's time to take a deep breath and switch on your PC to start organising your files there. As you go through, make sure that all your file names are super simple to understand with no obscure words or phrases that you won't be able to decipher later. And if you're someone who has a gazillion files on their desktop, now is the time to get these organised too as this will make you feel so much better every time you open up your screen. No more jumbled mess in front of you each time.

The final part of this de-clutter is to look at your emails. Now, this might bring you out in a cold sweat just thinking about it, but let me explain. If your email is causing you a problem, where you can't find what you need, or you're feeling stressed every time you open up your inbox, then you need to do something about it. If it doesn't trouble you and you're happy with how it's working for you, then don't bother.

If you're ready to de-clutter your inbox but the thought of it is too overwhelming, try blocking out 15 minutes a day for a couple of weeks. One idea is to set up your email folders first, then look at everything that would save you time in the long-run, like an automatic email signature, some frequently used mailing groups, and so on. Finally, go through your emails from the oldest to the most recent and either delete, action or archive in a folder. Set yourself a target of how many you're going to clear each day. You'll be amazed at how much you can get done with consistent small actions.

If getting organised is not something that comes naturally to you then this section might feel like a challenge. But it will no doubt give you the greatest rewards too.

- ☐ Desk
- ☐ Drawers
- ☐ Files
- ☐ PC Desktop
- ☐ E-mails
- ☐ Files
- ☐ File names

WHAT DOES YOUR DAY *REALLY* LOOK LIKE?

A big part of looking after your hat is ensuring you feel in control of your day, minimising those times when you're just treading water. If this is how you're feeling at the moment, getting to grips with what's going on in your day to make you feel this way will make a big difference.

When we're immersed in a situation, often we can't see the wood for the trees. We just keep going and keep going and keep going in the hope that one day it'll get better. All we're really doing here is getting used to working in that way. Pretty soon, it becomes the norm. In order for any change to happen to our day and for us to feel in control, we have to grasp the nettle and make something happen. But as you will most likely know, taking that first step to breaking the cycle of busy-ness can sometimes be tough. Especially if you don't know where to start.

In order to break out of this cycle and put in place the habits, processes and practices that you need to serve you and your day well, you first need to take time out to see what's actually going on and examine how you're spending your day.

A couple of questions on this...

What is it that keeps you so busy?

What hundreds of small tasks do you do that add up to your entire day?

Now, don't worry if you can't give me specific answers just yet. I want to explain where I'm heading with this.

So often our days will consist of lots and lots of tasks that we try to get done – all of which add up to our day. Some of these tasks may be things you've planned to do. Some of them may be interruptions from your team, phone calls, emails etc. And some might be spontaneous actions that have just popped up out of the blue. But until we can see our day laid out in front of us, it's much harder to see where we should be placing our efforts, and what we can do about all the little to-dos that sap our time and don't add any value whatsoever.

Only when we've got all the information can we devise systems that will be truly valuable to us.

One of the easiest ways to do this is to complete a Task Log.

You can download it here and full instructions on how to complete it at **www.barbaranixon.co.uk/bosshatfreebonuses**

For the next two or three days (or a week if you want a full accurate picture of everything you do), write down every little task that you're doing during your working day. And I mean *every* little task. Include the coffee breaks, interruptions (and what these interruptions are) and phone calls too.

To make it easier you can use the following key:

- I – Interruption (eg any unscheduled task)
- PT- Planned Task
- M – Meeting
- DT – Down time (This includes; social media; any unplanned admin; getting a coffee; chatting; texting; social call; reflection)

And make a note of how long each task takes.

Once you've completed your task log, review it by considering:

- Where you're spending most of your time

- What interruptions you're getting
- How many interruptions there are
- How many of the tasks that you're spending time on get you closer to your goals
- What tasks could have been dropped altogether or completed by someone else.

I know you're thinking that this will be Hell On Earth, but stick with me here. By digging deep and doing this for a few short days, you'll be able to pinpoint accurately exactly where your time is leaking and you can start cleaning it up. You'll see what your day *really* looks like – which might be a wake-up call – and where you need to be spending your time.

Once you've completed your log, you may see, for example, that you've developed a habit of spending the first hour of each day looking through emails, which on reflection isn't a good use of your time. You might fall into the social media trap every time you have a break; be scheduled for back-to-back meetings; get interruptions every 10 minutes, which is stopping you focusing on specific projects.

Whatever it is for you, make a note of it in your development plan as a focus area. As we go through the following sections, we'll address some of the more common time-wasting problems and cover what you can do about them.

Code (I;PL;M;DT)	Task	Time taken

Code (I;PL;M;DT)	Task	Time taken

Code (I;PL;M;DT)	Task	Time taken

IS YOUR TO-DO LIST HOLDING YOU BACK?

I've always been a big fan of the 'to-do' list. I used to list my way through the entire day, week, month and year, but then I realised that I was doing it all wrong. My 'to-do' list was actually holding me back.

Here's what happened. In my notepad, I had a list, a mile-long list, with everything that I needed to get done on there. But even though I had my trusted list by my side as I went through my day, I wasn't crossing off as much as I'd like. In fact, more often than not I was ending the day feeling hacked off that I hadn't done nearly as much as what I'd intended. And guess what. It was *always* because of 'other things' getting in the way. These are my most common excuses...

"If only I hadn't had all those interruptions."

"If only the phone didn't ring for a minute."

"If only I didn't get emails."

"If only I didn't have meetings."

"If only I didn't have so much to do."

"If only..."

You get the idea.

We can all spend time blaming everything else because we're not as productive as we'd like, but as with anything in life, there's always a common denominator. And that was me!

The real reason that I wasn't getting as much done was because I wasn't using my 'to do' list effectively at all. I was setting myself up to fail. I was planning far too much to do in the time I had available.

Here's what I mean.

Let's say I work for 8 hours, and I know that I want to have an hour for lunch (for easy maths' sake). That leaves me 7 hours of work.

Now, let's say I have 2 hours of meetings planned. I now have 5 hours of time for work.

Now, I know from my task log that on average I get an hours' worth of interruptions (again, for easy maths). I now have 4 hours of time available for work.

Then I looked at my 'to do' list and noted down roughly how long I thought each task would take me to do. No surprise, it was a lot more than 4 hours. In fact, more often than not I'd be writing down enough work in one day to get me through the week! No wonder I couldn't ever seem to get it all done.

Once I realised this, I started giving myself tasks to fit the time available and not the other way round. And my productivity soared.

Give it a try.

Write out what you want to get done this week ideally.

Now write down how much time (roughly) each task should take.

Now have a think about how much time you've got available to work on those tasks each day. Pick the tasks you need to do and can fit into the time available. For example, if you know you've got a report to write by a certain deadline and it's going to take an hour, that goes to the top of the pile and that's an hour gone. Make sense?

"It's about leaving work with a clear conscience and not a clear intray."

- (Unknown)

Once you have your tasks listed, time to get to work. Remembering to do any focus tasks when your brain is at its best, either the morning or in the afternoon, whatever it is for you.

One of my favourite productivity tips is Parkinson's law, which states "work expands so as to fill the time available for its completion". What this means is that, if you give yourself a week to write a report, it'll take a week. If you give yourself a day, it'll take a day.

Have you ever been in the position where a deadline has been moved forward dramatically and now all of a sudden you have a lot less time to do something than you did before? Or a huge order came in last minute? Or an important presentation suddenly needed to be done the next day when you thought you had a week?

Chances are you pulled out all the stops and got the job

done, right? There you go. This is why, when I'm working on a particular task that I need to focus on and get done, I set the alarm on my phone.

When I start a task, I put the time into the stopwatch on my phone and I get on with the work. Now, one of two things always happens. I'm so engrossed that when the alarm goes off I keep going until I finish or I beat the clock and finish ahead of time. Either way, win- win. If you get interrupted during that focus time, simply press pause on the alarm, and deal with the interruption before pressing start again.

When I first started doing this, my productivity shot through the roof. It helps you to focus on the task at hand and not get distracted.

Worth a shot, right?

Task	How long should this take?	Complete ☑

Task	Reason	**Rate 1-3 Did / Do you need to do this?** 1=No || 2= Someone needs to be trained || 3= Yes	Complete ☑

BLINKIN' INTERRUPTIONS!

Let's face it, as a Boss, you're going to be interrupted. It's just par for the course. You have a team, and from time to time, they're going to need you. When they do, you're going to get interrupted. Fact.

You also have a job to do, which will involve other people, who will on occasion want to contact you about things either by email or phone. So you will need to deal with these too. Fact.

For the most part, you need to accept that interruptions just come with the territory. They just do. You're never going to get rid of them all completely unless you start working in a cave.

That said, sometimes you do just need to be able to get your head down to get something done without someone wanting you for something. A great way to do this is to make sure you're not getting interrupted needlessly and that you've also got some boundaries in place. (Remember those rules you set up in the previous section when we talked about designing your hat?)

Let's start by having a quick check how often and why you get interrupted by reviewing your task log. Are there any patterns that have emerged? By patterns, I mean: are you always being asked the same question; are the questions connected by a similar theme or topic: are you being asked questions that you know for a fact that your team should know the answer to?

If so, time to re-think how you respond. When someone asks you a question, do you just answer it, solve the problem, or make the decision straight away? After all, why wouldn't you? Surely, it's far quicker that way. You've dealt with the query and everyone can now go on their merry way. Well, yes in theory, this would be the case, but in reality, all you're doing is teaching your team that when they show up with a query, you'll deal with it. So they keep doing it over and over again.

Let me give you an example.

Shoe laces are a bit of a pain, aren't they? Every parent in the world knows this (which is probably why Velcro was invented). It takes ages for a child to learn to tie their laces, and a painfully long time to wait for them to do it, especially when you're in a mad rush to get out the door and off to school in the morning. So what's the natural thing to do? Yep, you got it... to tie the laces quickly for them and then leg it to the school gates right? We've all done it. The problem is that all we're doing is getting them into the habit of having their laces done for them. So there's a period when you have to wait a reaaaaaallly long time for them to tie their laces before you can leave the house, but after a while, this timeframe gets shorter and shorter until they're doing it all by themselves without your help.

If this is where you are right now, have a go at pushing back a little bit. What I mean by this is, when a team member asks you a specific question that you know they should know the answer to, instead of just giving them the answer, ask them what they think they should do instead. This way, you're teaching them to be more solution-focused in the long run. It might not come easily at first. After all, you've also got into the habit of just sorting out the problem. You might find yourself feeling frustrated as interruptions start to take a bit longer, but hang in there and hold back. Even though you're coaching them, you're also re-training yourself too.

The other aspect to consider regarding interruptions is they may be highlighting a training need. Is the same question coming up time and time again? If this is the case, it might be that you could do some training for your team on this particular topic, or put a Frequently Asked Questions list on the company intranet or shared drive where everyone can access it.

Coaching your team to be more self-sufficient, and re-training yourself to not jump straight in with the solution does take time but is well worth the effort. Not only will you be empowering your team, you'll also be providing yourself with the time you need to be focusing on things that really do need your attention. There will be days when you just don't feel as though you have the patience (or the time) but give it a try and see how you go.

DO YOU FIND YOURSELF IN MEETING HELL?

If you sometimes find yourself going from meeting to meeting, simultaneously wondering how on earth you're going to find the time to complete any actions that come out of them, now's the time to do something about it.

Although meetings can be a massive time suck, they aren't always bad, provided they're managed correctly. They can be a great way of getting all the relevant stakeholders of a project around the table to make substantial moves forward.

Unfortunately, if they're not handled in the right way or run efficiently, they can easily be a rabbit hole to get lost in and can become a *fantastic* way to procrastinate and waste a tonne of time, rather than being productive and valuable.

If you can relate and know that meetings are not a good use of your time, take a moment to think of the reason why.

Ask yourself: what's the point?

With every meeting that you attend, ask yourself this simple question to decide whether it's a meeting that really requires your time or not. If there's no point going or you can't see what it is, go back to the organiser and ask them what they want to achieve.

There are times when meetings just seem to happen for the sake of it. And if that's the case, that meeting does not have to be taking up your valuable time. Instead, find out what the purpose is and decide if you need to be there. It may be that there simply needs to be a representative from your team or company, but is that a good enough reason to attend? And if so, does that person have to be you? It might not. In which case, look for someone else who can go in your place. Yes, you might need to spend a bit of time bringing them up to speed, but in the long run it'll free you up and be a great development opportunity for them.

Along the same lines of asking yourself what the point is, you can also have a think about what contribution you're expected to give. Make sure you see an agenda beforehand so you're aware of what's going to be covered, what you need to prepare in advance, and how long the meeting is going to take. If there's no agenda, again you can ask the meeting chair for one. Then during the meeting if you think the meeting has gone off-piste or it isn't being chaired effectively, you can use the agenda to get the group back on track.

Think about how you're booking your meetings

Having meetings back to back isn't much fun at all. Yes, you might prefer to get them all over and done with in the same day, but by the final meeting you'll be exhausted, probably hungry and not much use to anyone. Some people do prefer to have all of their meetings over and done with in one day or one part of the week, so it might be that Monday and Tuesday are your meeting days and then you know that the rest of the week is left free. If that's so, and it really works for you, then carry on, but try to arrange a short break in between so you can gather your thoughts, have a rest and a comfort break, or grab a bite to eat.

Can you use the phone instead?

Yes, it's nice to see someone face to face, but if you've got a busy day, it may more effective to pick up the phone and have a discussion rather than arrange a meeting. It's much quicker and more effective. It means that you don't have to go anywhere or worry about parking and all that stuff. You can also have the meeting via Skype or even jump on a conference call. This is getting more and more common, especially as we're speaking to people from all corners of the globe – so make the most of the technology that's available to you.

If possible, do all the reading beforehand

There's nothing worse than turning up at a meeting only to be handed loads of stuff that you've never seen before that someone is going to go through or you're now expected to read. Instead, speak to the chair and ask for any documents to be sent to you in advance so you can prepare properly. This keeps the meeting time down.

Do you have to be sitting down?

Having a meeting standing up is a fantastic way of keeping the energy levels raised and it works wonders for keeping the meeting running to time. It might not be a big favourite among everyone attending the meeting, but give it a go. Especially for those shorter meetings, as it's a good way of keeping it snappy.

Clamp down on devices

Ever been in the middle of a discussion and then felt the table vibrate because someone's mobile is buzzing? Not only is it distracting for everyone else, but it's distracting for the person receiving the call or email, as they're now thinking about the content of that message, rather than what's going on. Get everyone to keep their phones in their bags and stashed out of sight.

Take notes

Always keep track of anything you need to action as you go along, rather than wait for the minutes to hit your inbox.

It may take a while to get the minutes and you may be able to rattle off your actions quite quickly if you've got them to hand.

BEWARE THE DREADED MULTI-TASKING

Let me take a moment now to bust a big hairy myth. Multi-tasking doesn't work! There, I said it!

Over the years, I've met people who take great pride in being able to multi-task, but the proven reality is that it just doesn't work at all.

In fact, all it does is give you the illusion that you're getting loads done at once, when in reality you're not doing anything properly at all. All you're doing is skipping merrily from one task to another without doing any of it thoroughly, because you're not focusing. By multi-tasking, we're just taking our attention and focus away from where it's needed.

Have a think about where you tend to multi-task, and how it makes you feel at the time.

Now rather than multi-tasking for the next 24 hours, have a go at just doing one thing at once – mono-tasking if you like – and see how that goes.

Write down your results here...

HOW ARE YOU AT SAYING NO?

Saying no can be incredibly difficult. After all, we're conditioned to say yes, be helpful and supportive, and lend a hand. We might feel incredibly guilty when we say no to someone as though we're not being all of those things, or we worry that the other person will thinking badly of us if we refuse them... All of this is happening super-fast in your head and before you know it you've agreed to do something you really don't want to do that's going to take up your time. Then you're going to beat yourself up about it afterwards. Not only that, you're probably not going to put your all into it, as you really don't want to do it in the first place, which means you're not motivated. So, if you're not going to do it with 100% effort, why are you doing it at all?

Phew! I'm exhausted just thinking about it.

If this is you, then I can absolutely relate. I went through a phase where saying no was a bit of a problem for me and something that I had to address when I was volunteering to be on all sorts of committees. Usually, anything that had something to do with my children, like a club they were attending. I'd convince myself that someone had to do it, so it might as well be me. Before long, I found that every evening was filled up with yet another meeting or event. There was no longer any space (or energy) in my life for what needed to be done or that I enjoyed. It was then that I realised that something had to give. It was a harsh lesson but a much-needed one. Since then, I only say yes to requests I really want to take on, as we only have a finite amount of time.

"Tell me what is it you plan to do with your one and precious life."

- Mary Oliver

As I mentioned, when you find yourself saying yes to something you don't want to do, it's impossible to put your all into it. Ask a child to do something they don't want to do and more often than not they'll do it badly because they're not at all motivated. Their hearts aren't in it. As adults, we're no different. We go through the motions but deep down inside we're having a good old moan about it and being annoyed at ourselves for getting into this situation.

But here's the thing. There's no-one else to blame. We got asked and we said yes. That's the bottom line right there.

It's not the other person's fault for asking you. It's your fault for saying yes. So, how do you say no with confidence?

Be really clear about what you want to achieve

By understanding exactly what you want to achieve, whether that's for the day, the week, the month or even the year, you'll be able to pinpoint exactly what you need to do in order to reach your goals. Everything else that you get asked to do that falls outside of this – and doesn't help you achieve your goals – is a no. Maybe those requests aren't a no forever, but they're a no for right now. Either way, you've only got a certain amount of time in the day, week, month... If you don't want to do something, don't see the value in it, or even more importantly won't put your all into it, then it's a no and you can easily explain why.

Say no without saying no

If it's the word 'no' that you get hung up about, there are ways to say no without actually saying no. For example, you could say, "I'd love to help you with that, but I'm really busy with this at the moment, sorry".

See how that goes. Try saying no without saying no.

Put yourself in the other person's shoes

If you were asking someone to do something – and they genuinely couldn't do it – would you be okay with that? Chances are you would be, especially if they explained their situation to you. I know that we're all busy and we've all got stuff going on, so when someone says no to me that's totally fine. I'd rather they say no than try to do it and get stressed over it, or not want to do it, or even let me down later down the line. If I wanted them to help really badly, I'd go on to explain why, and I'd try to sell it to them. Maybe I'd explain how much of a priority it is. That's where some negotiation would come in and they could decide whether they're willing to help out on this occasion.

Same goes for you. Negotiate if they press you, but otherwise stick to your guns, because the other person is probably going to be alright with it.

Spend a few moments thinking back to when you said yes to something you really wanted to say no to.

- How did it feel?

- How else could you have dealt with this?
- What was the result?
- What are you dealing with right now that you should've said no to?

BUILD YOUR SYSTEMS

As I've mentioned, systems are incredibly important to keeping control of your day and making sure you're as effective as you can be.

You may already have some processes and systems in place that are used in your organisation. If this is the case, make some time to review them to ensure they're as effective as they can be. Sometimes systems are followed just because they've always been followed. That's fine, provided they're doing what they should be doing. But it never hurts to have a sense check every now and then to see if anything can be done easier, quicker, slicker or even cheaper. Now, I'm not talking about cutting corners here. I'm a big fan of processes being in place; however, I'm also a fan of ensuring the processes are reviewed regularly.

You might want to ask your team for feedback to see if there's an easier way to do something or whether your processes are working as they should. Remember, even though you're the Boss, answers don't always have to come from you.

Once you've reviewed your existing systems, take a look at your task log once again and see if anything is jumping out at you as something that could do with a system. For example, is there anything that can be automated; anything that takes a lot of time but could be quicker and easier if it were done differently; anything that could be communicated better to speed up a process?

Put your ideas in the box below and on your development plan to review later.

LOOKING AFTER YOUR HAT: A RECAP

Take the time to truly understand what you need.

If you haven't filled out all the exercises, here's a checklist of what we've covered and how you can be at your very best.

- Define your rules
- Identify your demons
- Understand what you bring to the party
- Stop comparing yourself to other people
- Research networking groups to join to expand your web
- Surround yourself with positive people
- Book time with yourself to reflect and plan
- Get organised
- Complete the task log to analyse your day
- Revamp your to do list
- Look at how you deal with interruptions
- Manage your meetings

- Watch out for multi-tasking
- Practice saying no
- Create processes that work for you

Well done, let's now move on to how to wear your hat with pride.

"Every single person has leadership ability. Some step up and take them. Some don't. My answer was to step up and lead"

– **Wilma Mankiller**

STEP 3: WEARING YOUR HAT

By now, you have designed your Boss Hat and put everything in place to look after it effectively. The next part of the puzzle is to learn how to wear it with confidence.

Now, I say 'learn how to wear it' because for some people this can be the most challenging part. I know we're only talking about a metaphorical hat here, but this is where you need to commit to stepping into the role, to claim it as yours, to take it up a level and own it.

As we're discovering, being a Boss isn't just about having the job title. It's not just about allocating tasks to ensure that everyone does what they need to do and managing performance. It's much more than that. It's about empowering and trusting others to do a great job, developing and growing people to achieve their potential. It's about motivating and inspiring teams to do their best in everything they do, creating a work environment where people thrive. It's about growing a team that not only supports each other but supports the business as well. And so much more...

And although most of this will happen as you go about your day-to-day work, it takes you committing to the role, to stepping up and to wearing your hat with pride.

There are some people in the world – you might be lucky enough to know one of them – who seem to have presence. These are the people who can hold a room. They walk in and people listen and take note. They are what some would call natural leaders. You know the type, right?

These are the people who *own* their role and are more than comfortable in their own skin.

What do these people have that others don't? How do they wear their Boss Hat with such ease and comfort? What is the difference between them and you?

Well, a lot of it comes down to confidence and experience. They didn't come out of the womb that way. They became that way as a result of experience and above all – and here's the secret – they made the decision that this was for them.

And this is for you too. You can absolutely feel the confidence to step into the role and wear your Boss Hat with pride. After all, it was made for you. No-one else. You've done the groundwork; now it's time to put it firmly on your head and own it. This doesn't mean being something you're not. It means being nothing other than yourself.

No-one on the planet has the same skills, the same personality, the same sense of humour and the same knowledge as you. You are unique. Completely and utterly unique in every single way. So embrace your uniqueness.

You don't have to pretend to be something you're not. You don't have to be a Jekyll and Hyde kind of Boss. What I mean by this is you don't have to be someone completely different in work than you are out of work. Yes, as we've already mentioned, you'll be a slightly different version of yourself, but that doesn't mean you have to change your personality completely. Be human. Be yourself. Your team will respect you all the more if they can relate to you. If they can see your personality shine through and if they can understand that you're doing things for the right reasons.

Stepping up and owning your role can be quite a daunting experience, especially when you have a team to manage. After all, how do you balance your needs and theirs too? The best way is to develop some key habits that you can do consistently. That way you can ensure you're doing the best for your team and getting the job done in a way that feels right for you.

Throughout this section I'm going to share 10 key skills that, when developed into habits and performed consistently, will go a long way to helping you do the best for your team and yourself.

Shall we start?

DAILY HABITS

Ah habits. Those pesky niggles that we seem to adopt when we're not trying and struggle to adopt when we try. Love them or hate them, they do have a purpose.

A habit is a great way of short-cutting all the nonsense in our brain. For instance, when we've got a habit, we no longer have to think about what we're doing; we just do it on autopilot. We can be thinking about other things while we're doing whatever it is that we've created a habit in. The more we do it, the easier and more effortless it becomes, which, provided it's a good habit, is great for getting productive.

There is loads of research around how long it takes us to adopt a habit. I've read articles that say it takes 30 days to make a habit. I've read articles that say it takes 60 days to make a habit, and there are probably lots of variables, like the person, the kind of habit, how committed you are. I know I've had experiences where I've struggled to make a habit (like going to the gym) and where a habit has just become second nature overnight, like when I became a vegetarian.

I don't remember spending time going for the meat options and then having to stop myself. I just remember committing to my new lifestyle choice. But maybe this was because I was really committed. That my 'Why' was stronger.

The Boss habits I'm about to talk about are key skills that you can weave into your everyday life, you may find some of them much easier to adopt than others and you might need to remind yourself to do it from time to time. You might even find yourself reverting to your old ways, falling off the wagon and just forgetting.. And that's okay. When that happens, just start again. Don't give up because 'you've failed' or it didn't work. And definitely no beating yourself up. Just remember what you're supposed to be doing and if it's working for you get back on it.

Now, I'm all about development without feeling overwhelmed so rather than attempt to incorporate all of these habits at once, instead read through them all and put them in order of what you think you need to focus on first in your development plan.

You might also want to get some feedback from your peers or your team to see what their thoughts are. Once you've decided what you're going to focus on, work on that one habit until you're happy that it's working for you and then move on to the next one.

HABIT #1 – BE A ROLE MODEL

Whether you realise it or not, as the Boss, your team are always watching and it's up to you to be the role model that they're looking for. It's human nature to behave in a way that other people behave. That's why role models are so powerful.

From when you enter the building until you go home at night, you're on show. Your team are looking to you for clues on how they should behave. It's perfectly natural, like I said. But here's the clincher. This book's about being a Boss that feels authentic to *you* so this next step is about doing what *feels* right too. That means always acting with integrity and in accordance with your values.

Being the Boss doesn't mean that you have to start power dressing (unless you want to) and be aloof. And it certainly doesn't mean trying to be something other than yourself. Your team will be able to spot that a mile off. Like this Boss who during work had the tendency to be controlling and overbearing and took great joy in micro-managing. Not someone you'd particularly enjoy working for, but outside of work he was the polar opposite.

Calm, happy, funny, outgoing, generous, you name it. He'd fallen into the trap of trying to 'be a Boss', whatever that meant for him, and it hadn't worked. Yes, his team liked him a bit more out of work but they didn't trust him at all. They couldn't relate to Jekyll or Hyde; they couldn't figure out what was real. Who was he really? Was the person at work the authentic version? Or the person in the pub?

Either way, his team were not on his side, and it wasn't until he started to show his true colours and be authentic, both in and out of work, that his team finally came on board.

Remember your uniqueness is your strength. Stand tall, be proud, dig deep and enjoy being you. You are the Boss – be the role model you were meant to be.

Habit #1 Top Tips

- Before you start, re-visit the first section, Designing Your Hat, to reflect on what you want from being a Boss and be honest with yourself. Are you already there? Are you doing this every day? How does it feel? You might also want to ask for some feedback from your team or your peers to get their thoughts.

- Take note of how you feel before you go into work. Are you feeling positive and confident? If not, try to capture these feelings before you head through the door. It might help if you check your body language too... Stand up tall, raise your head and smile.

- Be aware of your behaviours as you go about your day and make sure you're modelling the behaviours that you want from your team. For example, if you'd like your team to be positive... be positive. If you'd like your team to be professional... be professional. You get the idea.

- Share your stories with your team so they get to know the real you.

HABIT #2 – LISTENING

Listening, listening. Master this one and you'll be well on your way!

Listening is the number one exercise that you can do every single day that will always give you a return on your investment. Not only will you learn something, but you'll also make someone feel valued, and special. Best of all, it doesn't cost a thing!

The problem with listening is that we all think we can do it and that we're doing it all the time. But this isn't the case.

We can do a quick experiment right now. Think of the last time someone came up to you to say something. The very last time. What did they say? Can you remember exactly?

Chances are you can get the gist of what they said. But exactly the words they used? Probably not. The reason here is that most of us tend to listen at the very lowest level. Can we call this listening? Well, yes to a degree as we're listening out for things that'll spark our interest in some way or other. However, our mind is still off doing other things. Now, although this is listening in a sense and you're getting the top line of what's happening, you're not reaping any of the benefits. You're not really learning anything. And you're absolutely not making someone feel special, respected or valued, as they don't have your full attention. They can pick this up a mile off, believe me.

Let's take it a step further.

What are you doing when you say you're listening? Do you stop what you're doing and look at the person speaking or are you still tapping away at your keyboard?

Most of us, if we're being honest, have done the latter once or twice before. Is it making the other person feeling valued and special? Nope. Are you learning anything? Probably not. More to the point, what subliminal message are you sending out? That you don't really care; that you haven't got the time; that you're not interested; that they're not important. And on and on it goes.

By making listening a habit you can absolutely make a positive change to the way you manage others and how they feel.

The easiest way to make listening a way of life is to make the *commitment* to listen. By that I mean, when someone comes to speak to you, stop what you're doing and focus on them. Completely. They'll instantly feel as though you're listening to them. You'll be making it much easier to focus on them without getting distracted by other things.

Now, before I continue, I know what you're thinking...

"But Barbara, I haven't got time to be stopping what I'm doing every single time someone comes to my desk. I'd never get anything done. And I really don't want someone to take root at my desk and just keep talking."

I hear you.

Sometimes it's just not a good time to be breaking off from your task to listen to someone. That's where honesty comes in. Simply explain that this isn't a great time as you're busy with something else. Suggest they come back at [give them a time] when they'll have your full attention.

This way, you've still listened to their initial query and you've still made them feel valued, but you're simply explaining that you haven't got the time right now. The word of caution here is this: if you specify a time, you must make sure you keep it.

Otherwise, any trust you have gained will soon go out the window.

The second way to improve your listening is to show it through your body language. Your body language is key to building rapport with other people, which then leads to trust.

By working to show the other person that you're listening, you're helping yourself listen, as you're improving your focus. But in order to do this we must first think about how we're coming across to the other person.

Let me tell you a story.

Years ago, I was having a one-to-one with a member of my team, when they gave me the feedback that they felt uncomfortable sharing ideas with me as I always look so angry.

I was stunned. I love new ideas and I certainly didn't feel angry. But that's when I realised that as I was listening I was screwing up my face. In my head, I was concentrating, but my listening face was being misconstrued as an angry face. Once I knew about this I made every effort to change my 'listening face' to help the people who I was listening to.

Listening is a skill that takes practice, but it's so worth the effort. Even if you find it exhausting at first.

The secret to listening is to stop what you're doing and really focus on that other person and what they're saying to you. Try not to worry about what you're going to say next.

Use eye contact and gestures that show you're listening. Then use their words when you reply so they know that you understand what they're saying.

A point to remember here is to not be afraid of silences. We're hard-wired to fill in silences as quickly as possible. That's when we stop listening, because we're busy thinking of the next thing to say to avoid a silence. Instead of rushing to fill the silence, train yourself to just wait. The other person might continue to speak or you'll come up with the right question or reply that suits that moment. Either way, silence is no bad thing!

Now, although body language can be incredibly powerful to show that we're listening, it can often work the other way too, especially as we don't often realise how we're coming across or what our body language is saying. So, my challenge to you is to get some feedback.

Ask your team how you come across when you're listening to them.

Ask a close colleague to give you some feedback on how you come across when you're listening to someone in meetings or in the office.

Examples of some questions worth considering...

- Do you have a habit of gazing into the distance when someone is talking to you?
- Do you (like I did) screw up your face?
- Do you have a habit of stroking your beard or curling your hair?
- Do you tap or click your pen?
- Do you find yourself sighing or rolling your eyes?

These are just some examples of how habits in your body language can be affecting your listening skills and how others perceive you. Ultimately, this body language is affecting your rapport with people and feedback could prove to be invaluable, as something small and simple might be stopping someone from thinking that you're paying attention.

Habit #2 Top Tips

- Stop what you're doing and look at the person speaking to you. Really try and focus on what they're saying.
- Be aware of every time you want to interrupt and try to stop yourself from doing this even if you're in a rush.
- Practise listening everywhere you go, not just at work. See how much you can remember of what someone has said to you.

HABIT #3 – BE CURIOUS

A few years ago, I was talking to the managing director of a successful company about what his number one leadership tip was. This is what he said...

"Never stop being curious."

I loved this!

Having a healthy level of curiosity is important when you're leading a team, so that you're not only keeping your finger on the pulse, but you're also encouraging debate and discussion, initiating problem-solving and creativity, empowering people, and enabling your team members to share the progress they've made, celebrate their successes, and ask for support should they need it.

Curiosity does all of this. All it takes is a combination of great questions and good listening.

Note here that I'm talking about 'healthy curiosity'. This is where you'll need to walk the tightrope between being curious and being a micro-manager.

What we're looking for is trust-building by asking questions and listening to the response on a regular basis. This doesn't mean questioning every move someone makes or not empowering them to do anything themselves.

The former builds trust and a healthy working environment, while the latter only serves to create an environment where people feel stifled, suffocated and disempowered. Where would you rather work?

So, how do we walk this tight rope?

Being empowered in a role is a great gift to give someone. It means that they're trusted to do the job that they were given, that they are a valued member of the team, that they are supported should they make a mistake, and more to the point, that they are capable.

When you recruit a new team member, you are ultimately saying to them that they can do the job and that, in return, they'll receive a salary, benefits and so on. They may need additional training, support, and most definitely an induction to get them up and running, but in the main, they are capable of doing what they were brought in to do.

Then comes the hard part – trusting them to do the job.

In order to empower someone, we have to trust them, and sometimes this can take a while to establish. Sometimes we're so used to doing the tasks ourselves or in a certain way, it can be difficult to let go. In fact, for many Bosses, this is the most challenging habit of all – learning to let go and allowing your team to do the job that they're paid to do.

How do you empower your team? Set clear objectives with each person in the team so you both know what the individual is working on. This will help when you're getting updates on projects going forward.

Set up regular meetings with each person in your team to get updates on where they are. This could be once a month, once a fortnight or even once a week depending upon the project. As long as it happens when you've arranged it, that's the most important part – trust again. Over time, that meeting will become a valuable place to share ideas, gain insights and for both parties to ask questions.

Have a regular team meeting. Again this could happen once a month or once a quarter depending upon the needs of your team. It will serve as a great way to communicate as a group. It's also a way for the whole team to collaborate and bounce ideas around.

Be visible. As tempting as it might be to hide away in your office or at your desk and just get on with your work, it always pays to be visible. What I mean by this is to take the time to check in with people throughout the day; have a wander round to make sure you've touched base with the team; spend a few moments chatting with the team to see how they are and a bit of social chat. All of this helps to show your team that you're approachable and available.

Habit #3 Top Tips

- Reflect on these questions. How empowered is your team? How empowered do the individuals feel? Is there anything more you can do? Is there anything that's holding them back?

HABIT #4 – OWN YOUR VOICE

Stepping up can be scary at times, especially if you're in new territory. One of the scariest parts is having the courage to speak up and be heard.

As I type this, I remember my Theatre Studies teacher back when I was 16 shouting at us "have the courage of your convictions" whenever we were mumbling in class. And even now, years later, I have never forgotten that.

Fast forward a few years and I remember having a chat with my then-Boss about speaking up in meetings. I recall wanting to say something, but not having the courage. I'd keep it to myself and the moment would pass. I'd always leave meetings feeling annoyed with myself for not speaking up. His advice was simple, "Speak up. Your voice and opinion are valuable." So I did, but it still didn't come easily. In fact, I always felt I was forcing myself.

Fast forward a few more years and I was having the very same conversation with Dave, my husband. By then, I was fine speaking in front of people, but then I was put on a committee of about 40 people covering a topic that wasn't my area of expertise. My old issue of not speaking up raised its head once more. Dave, as always being the voice of wisdom, said three simple words to me, "12 Angry Men".

"What?!"

"*12 Angry Men*. It's a good film. You should watch it. It's about a man who's on trial for murder. All but one of the jury, are ready to convict him and it's about how this one person speaks up... *12 Angry Men*. You've got a voice. Use it. What's the worst that could happen?"

And he was right. What's the worst that could happen? From that moment on, I've never been afraid of owning my voice. You've got a voice. Use it.

Habit #4 Top Tips

- Practice makes this so much easier (and eventually perfect). Seize every opportunity to speak in front of your team. Whether that's a briefing session at the start of the day, at team meetings or on conference calls. Eventually it'll become second nature.

HABIT #5 – BE CONSISTENT, NOT A MAGPIE

You're busy working away when suddenly an email pops up. What do you do? Ignore it and carry on with what you're doing? Click on it?

Be honest!

If you clicked, chances are the answer to 'are you a magpie?' would be a big fat yes. You're attracted to shiny things. These might be emails, interesting documents that land on your desk, something that's happening at the other end of the office, or anything else that could distract you.

If this sounds like you, you are definitely not alone.

I have fought 'magpieness' for years. (Yep, it's a word now!) And I know what it feels like. The problem here is that although you might be attracted to the next shiny object, your team needs consistency.

"Consistency is not an accident"

- (Unknown)

To build up trust, they need to know what to expect from you, and also what you expect from them. They'll also need to understand that when you set a deadline or call a meeting, it's going to go ahead. You don't want them thinking you've created something just in case nothing 'more important' crops up.

How you behave is a catalyst for the rest of the team. If you behave in a magpie fashion, being reactive to everything, then so will your team. If you cancel meetings at a moment's notice, then so will your team. If you don't follow processes or you cut corners on systems, then guess what. So will your team.

As well as sending out a clear message that this behaviour is acceptable, it indicates that whatever gets bumped isn't that important.

For instance...

If you commit to doing regular one-to-one reviews with your team and then start cancelling them.

If you create your communication strategy to include daily briefings and monthly team meetings and they stop happening.

If you start a project, get the team motivated and then move on to the next thing before it gets finished.

If you set a deadline and then don't keep it.

If you insist on something being important and then lose interest.

Before long, people will assume that they don't matter either. You might not think that those 30-minute catch up sessions with your team matter that much – but for the individuals, they might matter a lot. And there goes the trust that you've spent time building up.

Consistency matters

The problem here for natural magpies is that there's a real danger of boredom setting in. It's hard to remain consistent when you're struggling to motivate yourself. More importantly, how can you motivate your team when you're not feeling it?

Just like any member of your team, you need to keep motivated too. You are human after all, so put in that support mechanism for yourself.

This is where your why comes back into play.

Take a moment now to think about where you lose interest in your role.

- Where do you get bored?
- Where have you lost motivation?
- Where do you know you'll struggle to be consistent?

Once you've done that, re-visit your why that you completed in the first section Designing Your Hat and the exercise 'What do you want to be like as a Boss?' to remind yourself of what's important to you. Then spend a few moments creating a mini 'why' for each of the regular tasks that you have in place. Why did you set them up in the first place? What is the benefit? How do they add value? As you're doing this, if the task has no real importance, or reason to be done then it can get bumped without any time being wasted.

Are you the best person?

Although you're a magpie, you might have someone in your team who is not, and who loves regular tasks and logical processes to follow. If that's the case, have a think whether you're the best person to be doing the task or if it's something you can gladly pass on to someone who would do a much better job.

Habit #5 Top Tips

- Keep an eye on your magpie tendencies and notice when you get distracted most.
- Plan regular tasks in advance and get them in the diary with a note saying – *do not move!*
- There may be some tasks that you find mundane. Although they still have to be done, they don't have to be done by you. Find the person who you can delegate these tasks to and free up your time for other things.

HABIT #6 – NURTURE PEOPLE

I remember when I had one of my first jobs. I really didn't like it. Before long, I started to dislike Sundays too because Monday came next. I wasn't motivated *at all* and desperately didn't want to go into work each morning. Even though, I tried to make the best out of it – really and honestly – I couldn't wait to leave of an evening.

But it didn't end there. As time went on, it started to leak into other areas of my life. Because I wasn't motivated at work, I found it harder to be motivated at home, and I didn't want to do anything that I normally enjoyed. I just couldn't be bothered. The energy was sapped out of me. What I did have time for, though, was moaning about it. I'm the type of person that has to vocalise what's on my mind. I don't sit stewing in a corner. I talk about things that bother me. And this is exactly what I did. But I turned into a real moaner! Not a natural state for me to be in. As a glass-half-full kind of girl, for me to moan on and on is telling that I wasn't in the best place.

Luckily, I soon got fed up enough of this moany me and did something about it. I found a new job and got the heck out of there. In hindsight, though, I'm pleased to have had the experience of having been in that state. Because during that time I realised a great deal.

1. A Boss matters.

Just because we have to work – which we all do – doesn't mean it has to be horrendous. Work can and should be good for us. It should energise us. It should motivate us, because our work should matter. I've since been fortunate to have worked places that did just that. Where I've given my all to my work from morning until evening. And even though I was shattered I was 'good' shattered. I was pumped. I was motivated. I left knowing that what I'd done meant something and had added value. I left buzzing. This in turn affected the rest of my life. I went home with the same incredible energy. My family noticed. My personal life benefited in spades. This is what I wanted every day to be like. To be filled up with a positive vibrant awesome energy that I could then pass on to everyone I touched.

Your role as a Boss is to be able to look yourself in the mirror and know that you've done everything you could to bring out the best in someone. To empower them. To ensure that as they head home every evening, they're spending time with their loved ones, not moaning about you or their work.

Have a think about how you can motivate your team and increase the positive energy. Make a note of your ideas here.

2. Again, a Boss matters!

We want to be seen. No-one truly wants to go through life invisible. We want someone to notice us. We want to be invested in, mentored, recognised.

A good Boss can do just that. They take the time to notice. And not just what could go wrong and not just the mistakes. But the million other things that happen during the work day, what goes well, where magic has happened. The effort from the team. The smiles across the room. The laughter, the fun. The fundraising. The making tea for other people. The great customer service. The hustle and the bustle. The birthday cakes. The impossible order completed. The awkward customer appeased. The new customer. The pitch. The presentation. The questions. The learning. The teaching. The pitching in. The helping each other out. The cleaning. The standards kept. The new people welcomed. The praise. The humming as people work. The radio playing. The 'mornings' and the 'have a good nights'. The 'thanks for today, see you tomorrows'. The noticing that people really do care.

Make these magnets for your attention. Notice the great big enormous things, yes. Zoom in on what everyone gives. But remember too that the small things matter. Even little things make a difference.

Spend a day noticing all the great things that are happening in your team. Make a note of them here.

- Who have you not spoken to in a while?
- Who is going un-noticed?

Make a note of what you're going to do to make this a habit.

3. Everyone should know how they fit.

You're not in the habit of paying people for things that you don't need. Every single role makes a difference to the overall picture. As I write this, I'm reminded of a story of Kennedy going to visit Nasa. During his visit he has the pleasure of speaking to lots of different people all working tirelessly to put a man on the moon. Astronauts and scientists. Then on the way back to the car Kennedy walks down the corridor and comes across a man mopping the floor. He stops and asks the man, 'What do you do here?' The man mopping the floor replies, 'I'm helping put a man on the moon, Sir.'

When everyone knows their place and the part they play, they can play their part with pride and excellence. And above all... feel valued.

Ask yourself:

- What's the vision for your company?
- What's the vision for your team?

Find out if everyone knows the part they play. Come up with ideas to break down any barriers in your team so everyone knows the value of each other too.

4. The small stuff matters.

You are a human being, surrounded by other human beings. You might be the Boss, but you are not *THE BOSS*. You're just a person like everyone else. And that means people notice the small stuff you do. Let me explain. This Boss got things done. His team was consistently at the top end of the sales scoreboard and they were doing great. For the most part, he was terrific to work for. The only problem was that when he walked into work at the start of the day he didn't say 'good morning' to a single soul. He marched on past them to his desk. And *even though* he was great at everything else, his team couldn't let this go.

Another Boss was again a great person to work for. Her team loved her. She was there for everyone and her team were flying. Her problem? She never got the coffees. Ever. Not once. And this drove her team bonkers.

When I was a little girl, my dad was an electrician working on water treatment sites. This meant that he was outside in all weathers working in the Yorkshire Dales. Anyway, at the time he was working for a guy who never, ever forgot his birthday. Every year, even after this guy retired and didn't work with my dad anymore, a birthday card landed on our mat for my dad. And every year, my dad would say to me, “That’s the sign of a great Boss”. There was no more money. There were no more benefits. No additional holidays. Just a card. And it meant the world!

The small stuff oh-so matters!

- Do you know everyone’s birthday?
- When was the last time you got the drinks?
- Do you know how everyone takes their tea/coffee?
- Do you say ‘good morning’, ‘goodnight’ and ‘thank you’?

Habit #6 Top Tips

- Take time to notice everyone in your team. You might think that they're ok and just getting on with it, but they may need a bit of TLC from time to time. Put reminders in your diary to catch up with everyone on a regular basis.

- Put a note in your diary of when birthdays are, or if there's a special occasion coming up for people so you don't forget. Make a note of how everyone likes their tea/coffee and stick it near the kitchen to help you remember.

HABIT #7 – ACT WITH INTEGRITY

We all have our values, and we all have an invisible line between what we deem to be right and wrong. Most if not all of us have also had that uncomfortable feeling of treading too close to the 'other' side of that line.

"No matter what, you always have to be able to look yourself in the mirror."

Just because we're the Boss doesn't mean we have to be the same as every other Boss in the business. You're not a clone. You're unique with your very own sense of what's right. You have your own opinion and a voice. You don't have to follow suit if something doesn't sit right.

"Just because your friends jump off a bridge doesn't mean you have to"

– (everyone's mum)

But you are the Boss.

You do have to step up and act in the interests of the business, make decisions that may not always be popular, but that have to be made, and follow through on the ones you stand by.

You do have to own it. There's no-one else to blame. The buck stops with you. If something's not right, it's up to you to do something about it.

You build up trust and maintain it through honesty.

You know that at the heart of everything is good communication.

You act in the best interests of the business – and that means everyone *in* the business too.

You say no when you need to and feel comfortable doing just that.

You act with integrity.

Habit #7 Top Tips

- Follow your instincts. You'll know deep down if something is the right thing to do. If you're struggling to zone in on your inner voice take some time out to sit and be still to have a think, and reflect.

HABIT #8 - SHARE AND COLLABORATE

In one of my first ever jobs, I had the great pleasure of watching a keynote speaker. Sadly, I've long since forgotten his name but his message has always stayed with me.

He explained that for many years he worked at a manufacturing plant on the same piece of machinery. He then took a year-long sabbatical and when he came back he discovered that the machine he looked after had been changed.

"What's happened to the machine?" he asked his manager.

"We swapped it. Things change."

"I get that", the man said, "but what's upset me is that what was wrong with the old one is exactly the same as what's wrong with the new one. If you'd asked me about it, we could have really moved on."

The people who work the job know the job. Keep them in the loop. Communication is key. Share as much as you can. Involve your teams with decisions and new ideas. Empower individuals to come up with their own solutions. Keep them in the know on everything that's going on.

No-one needs a 'them and us'. A business with barriers and blocks is not a healthy place to work. Word by the jungle drums rarely tells the truth. Create a culture of inclusivity and leap forward together.

Your communication strategy forms a key part of your daily habits. Take a look at the checklist below to see where you need to be focusing on your communication and have a think about how it can work for you.

- Do you have regular team meetings? yes/no
- Do you have regular one-to-one meetings? yes/no
- Do you have a regular time of day/week when you catch up with your team? yes/no
- Do you have an internal newsletter or intranet? yes/no
- Do you post updates on a notice board, or a platform? yes/no
- Do you have a system for capturing ideas and feedback? yes/no
- Do you ask your team if there's anything that can be done

better or improved on? yes/no

- Do you keep your team in the loop with the business? yes/no

What is your communication strategy going to look like?

Habit #8 Top Tips

- The more people know, the more they'll feel a sense of ownership and ability to share ideas and feedback. Find a way of keeping your team in the loop that works for you. If in doubt, ask them what they want and need to know.

HABIT #9 – PRAISE AND THANKS

It's human nature to want to feel appreciated and valued. The more we feel this way, the more we'll do to be appreciated and valued.

If you've ever been around children, you'll see this every day. When you praise a child for doing something well, they will continue the same behaviour as they'll want your approval.

Your team is no different. I appreciate that they're not children, nor should they be treated as such, but saying 'thank you' and 'well done' for a job done well should absolutely be worked into your day.

Through my career, I've discussed praise many times over with the people I've worked with. Quite often the same response comes up, which look like: fear that if they praise their team all the time, it will soon start to come across as disingenuous; feeling fraudulent and a fake; looking like they have some hidden agenda.

Here's my take on this.

Your team probably spend more time with you than they do with their own families and friends. During this time, they'll be working their butts off. They might have done something to move them further towards their goal. Maybe they've finished a project they've been working on or they've sorted out a particularly awkward customer complaint. Maybe they've moved Heaven and Earth to put an order together. Maybe they started early and stayed late, or maybe they've consistently delivered every single day without a fuss. Whatever it is, saying thanks to your team matters. Ignoring them and assuming that they know that they've done a good job will only breed resentment. Everyone wants to feel appreciated. So say it! A quick thanks seems small, but it'll mean the world, and when it comes from the heart with the right intention, it'll never come across as anything but genuine.

It's worth mentioning that recognition doesn't always have to come from you. It will be just as powerful when team members are cheering each other on. This is something you can encourage, maybe as a part of your regular team meetings, where you celebrate any recent successes and achievements.

If you do this consistently, before long it will become part of the team's DNA to support, praise and encourage each other.

That not only becomes a great motivator for all members of the team, but creates a team where everyone feels valued. Let's face it, that's just created a *great* place to work.

How can you build in ways to celebrate success that feels right for the team?

Habit #9 Top Tips

- Keep a check on how many times you've praised someone or said thanks. Don't assume that everyone knows they're doing a good job and that you appreciate them, find a way to tell them.

HABIT #10 – SEEK OUT FEEDBACK

There are some things that just go with the territory – and one of these is giving feedback. But what about getting it? How are you are actively seeking out feedback?

Feedback doesn't have to be a one-way street and it doesn't have to just come from above. In fact, some of the best (and most honest) feedback can come from your team.

How often do you ask your team for feedback? And if you don't, why not?

Feedback can be incredibly powerful as it can help you understand more about yourself, how you behave, how you come across and how others perceive you. But what's key is how it's received.

Yes, it can be hard to hear someone say you need to improve in some way, especially if it's delivered quite bluntly. But take it on the chin and see if it's something you want to take notice of. You don't have to take notice of every little bit of feedback, but sometimes you might just learn something that comes in handy.

Have a go at asking your team for feedback. You might want to kick off by asking them whether there's anything you can do better.

Habit #10 Top Tips

- Start small by asking your team if there's anything more they need from you, or if there's anything you can improve on at the end of a one to one meeting.

WEARING YOUR HAT: A RECAP

Habit #1 – Be yourself

Be aware of when you're feeling uncomfortable or shrinking in your own skin. Make a note of it and practice standing tall and being proud of your role.

Habit #2 –Listening

Stop what you're doing and focus on the other person.

Make eye contact.

Be aware of your body language and how you're coming across.

Get some feedback about how others feel when you're listening to them and about how you come across in terms of your body language when you're listening.

Habit #3 – Be curious

Set clear objectives with each person.

Have a regular one-to-one with each member of your team.

Have a regular team meeting.

Practice asking open questions.

Be visible.

Habit #4 – Own your voice

Practice speaking up in meetings.

Habit #5 – Be consistent

Create a motivation strategy for yourself.

Create a list of recurring tasks and create a system to help you ensure you're consistent with them.

If necessary, delegate tasks you struggle to maintain.

Habit #6 – Nurture people

Think about each member of your team and understand what

motivates them.

Spend time noticing all the great things that are happening in your team.

Make sure your team members understand the vision of the company and the team.

Create a list of ideas to break down any barriers that may exist in your team.

Make a list of the 'small stuff' like everyone's birthday and how they each like their tea/coffee.

Make sure you say 'morning', 'night' and 'thanks' each day.

Habit #7 – Act with integrity

Look for ways to continuously build up trust.

Be honest always.

Habit #8 – Share and collaborate

Create a communication strategy that works for your team.

Habit #9 – Praise and thanks

Get comfortable at praising your team.

Thank your team each day.

Habit #10 – Seek out feedback

Regularly ask your team for feedback on how you can improve.

Great work – Now you've got your hat firmly on your head, let's explore how to pass it on.

"

Human resources are like natural resources; they're often buried deep. You have to go looking for them, they're not just lying around on the surface. You have to create the circumstances where they show themselves.

"

– Ken Robinson

STEP 4: PASSING ON THE HAT

Sometimes the biggest failing we can make as a Boss is to believe that we have to know everything or be all things to all people. This is one of the biggest Boss myths there is. It simply isn't true.

Your job isn't to be the font of all knowledge. It's not to try to do everything yourself. In fact, trying to live up to that is the quickest route to feeling completely inadequate, out of your depth and exhausted. Yes, you may know how to do everything and yes you may have even set up the processes and systems, but this still doesn't mean that you have to do it yourself, because that's why you have a team.

Your team are there for a reason. Without them, there would be no business and no reason for you to be there. You hired them for a purpose. Provided you hired the right people, your job is to allow them not only to do their job, but also to develop and grow as you and the business grow. This is what passing on your Boss Hat is all about. To develop your team, as well as allowing yourself to delegate, trust, empower and step away, giving you room to develop and grow as well.

This is not something to feel threatened by.

You don't have to worry about being passed by or overtaken by other people beneath you. You should never worry about your team knowing more than you. To be able to lead people, you don't need to know absolutely everything. Gone are the days where a Boss needs to be able to do the jobs of each of their team members.

Instead, feel confident in the knowledge that you have permission to lead the team without feeling inferior or like you're lacking in some way. Your job as the Boss is to lead, not to be able to do every single task or be involved in every single issue.

Think of any successful leader in history. They consciously surround themselves with brilliant people, experts in their fields, so that they don't have to do, or know, everything. It's exactly the same for you.

Your team is there to take the strain from you. To be the experts. To be your support. Your job is to help the individuals in your team to do that.

You at your best isn't being involved in everything. You at your best isn't rushing from pillar to post trying to be the master of all things. You at your best isn't about feeling stressed or overwhelmed. You at your best isn't about suffocating your team. You at your best isn't about keeping your team in place, while you maintain control. And you at your best isn't about you working all hours God sends while your team leaves on time and relaxes on a weekend, as you're still slaving away.

Passing on your hat isn't about passing on the baton and retiring. It's about having the confidence to keep on moving upwards. You are only as strong as your team.

Give yourself room to breathe. Give your team room to grow. And give yourself the opportunity to step up even further by passing on your hat.

HELP OTHERS GROW

At the start of my career, I had the pleasure of working at a large company helping out with an induction where there was a large number of brand new managers. At the time, the CEO came to speak to them and what he said has stuck with me ever since.

"As a manager your job is to help other people get where you are."

As soon as he said that, I understood perfectly that the best Bosses don't hold people back; they help them grow, because when they grow, everyone grows.

"A rising tide lifts all boats"

– (John F. Kennedy)

Your team has a wealth of hidden talents that you probably know nothing about. Talents, experience and skills that may be as yet untapped. They're just waiting for you to uncover them. They may have skills that they have acquired in previous roles, or attributes from positions they've held as part of their hobbies, but are just not using in their current role.

Everyone has so much more in their arsenal than what you see on a day-to-day basis. It's your job to uncover the gold that's buried beneath their tough exterior. And the best way to do that is to get to know your team.

You may have worked with your team for a while already, but how well do you know them? Sometimes when we've worked with someone for a while, we find ourselves thinking of them in a certain way, pigeon-holing them or tarring them with a certain brush, depending upon how they were in the past. But people change and evolve, just like you, and they should be given the benefit of the doubt, room to grow, and an opportunity to change.

You've shared your story. Now it's time to get to know theirs too.

- Spend time getting to know your team.
- What do they do outside of work?
- What roles have they done previously?
- What do they want to do in the future?

- What tasks would they like to have a go at?
- What are they good at?

What did you learn?

When you've learnt more about your team, you can then move on to actively developing them. It's worth mentioning that not everyone wants to develop into something that they perceive to be bigger. Some people are more than happy coming in to work, doing their job, and going home again. And that's perfectly okay too. Developing people doesn't have to mean getting them ready for their next role or giving them completely new skills. It can be helping them to be the very best they can be in their current role. It can be increasing their confidence or utilising their skills and experience by asking them to help others.

This also isn't about setting up a formal development plan for your team (although that is always a helpful tool). Instead, it's about you making a habit out of seeing opportunities for people to develop, stretching their comfort zones, and getting them to continuously develop and grow.

Take a few moments to look around your team and think of at least one way per person that you could help them develop. Is it a task that you can delegate? A project that they can get involved in? A meeting that they can start to attend? Other people who they can help train? An additional responsibility? Or just to empower them to do their job and give them the praise they need?

Make a note of them here and then find time to have a chat to them about it. By keeping development always on the agenda, your team will start to feel more confident about speaking to you when they want to do or learn something new.

TAKE THE LEAP AND DELEGATE

Be honest... Have you ever found yourself saying these words?

"It's quicker if I do it myself."

You've got something to do. Something that you always have to do and have always done. You've got into a groove, but if you were completely honest, it's not the best use of your time. And if you were being really really honest, you don't even like doing it all that much. But it still needs to be done.

It doesn't have to be done by you!

Yes, it's quicker if you do it yourself, but then you'll always be doing it. It's always going to be on your to-do list. So surely it makes more sense to train someone else to do it, help them get the hang of it, support them if they need you to and then let them get on with it.

This is a case for my mantra 'short-term pain for long term gain'.

Spending some time developing someone else will pay off in

dividends. But before you leap in and start handing over loads of tasks let's set some clear ground rules here.

1) Make a list and start small

Make a note of all the tasks that you're regularly doing that could easily be done by someone else and see how much time they're taking up. (You'll probably be surprised at how much time this really is and what you could get done instead.) Once you've got your list, decide which of the tasks you're going to delegate first. Then go work on that.

2) Take time to train

Rather than just jumping in and delegating a task, make sure your team member is fully trained. By taking the time to go through this properly, you'll be building your own confidence that they know what to do, but you're also ensuring that they're happy with what they need to do too. This is the step where most people fall down as the good old 'it's quicker if I do it myself' comes into play. The thing is, if you skimp on this, neither of you will feel happy about doing the task. Then the chances of either the team member failing or you just doing it anyway are much higher.

Remember, doing this step gives you back up and means that you can focus on other matters going forward. Short-term pain, long-term gain!

3) Have regular reviews

Build in some regular checkpoints so that you know everything is as it should be. This doesn't have to be something that happens on a long-term basis for smaller tasks, but it's a good way to build up confidence, and gives you the ability to spot any mistakes early on.

Have a think of some of the tasks that you do on a regular basis that you could delegate.

PASSING ON YOUR HAT: A RECAP

As you grow so should the people around you in your team. Have a go at the following exercises if you haven't done them as you've been reading:

- Get to know your team and learn about their hidden talents
- Detach yourself from tasks that you've been doing that you can delegate and start passing them on
- Trust and empower your team to do a great job

NOW WHAT?

Welcome to the world of embracing your uniqueness. You're now ready to start sharing it with the world and being the Boss you were meant to be. A Boss that can absolutely get the very best out of themselves and others.

You care...

You make a difference...

You matter... You really do.

You don't just do a job. You do a great job. But you knew that already, because you're here, and you're already on your own journey.

I'm so glad that you've included me in it.

If you've not seen them yet, there are some bonuses especially for you waiting at **www.barbaranixon.co.uk/bosshatfreebonuses**

And if you'd like to continue your Boss Hat journey for you or your teams, visit **www.barbaranixon.co.uk**

I'd love to hear your Boss Hat stories. Please do email me at:

boss.hat@barbaranixon.co.uk

"BE THE BOSS WHO MAKES A DIFFERENCE TO SOMEONE."

ABOUT THE AUTHOR

Barbara Nixon is a coach, trainer and writer who helps managers and leaders get the very best out of their teams and themselves. She works with organisations to develop their leadership teams through one-to-one coaching and designing and delivering programmes, all with an emphasis on relevance, and easy application.

With nearly 20 years in learning and development, the first 12 years of which was spent working in training departments of two large UK retailers, Barbara is passionate about managers and leaders being the key to success in any organisation. She helps them to lead from a place that's authentic and people-focused whilst at the same time helping them to achieve their own potential.

As an avid writer, Barbara shares more on these topics at **www.barbaranixon.co.uk**. She has also been featured in

Addicted2Success, *Training Zone* and *MMB Magazine The modern working mothers website*, and is a resident webinar broadcaster for *Shorebird*.

When not working Barbara spends her time with her husband Dave, their four children and their dog in Yorkshire in the UK, and loves walking, growing veg (to varying degrees of success!) and travelling.

Connect with Barbara

Website: www.barbaranixon.co.uk

Facebook: barbaranixonleadershipcoach

Twitter: Bnixon

Linkedin: barbaranixon1

APPRECIATION

The idea for this book has been in my head for many years, and the goal to write it has been on my list for every New Year's Eve since. Finally in 2016, the universe probably got fed up of me repeating myself and brought me a few people that all in their own way gave me the nudges (or shoves) to actually get it done!

And here's where I give them the credit they really deserve.

Kris Emery, thanks for the well-timed email nudge, and for sharing your brilliance when it came to editing this book. I really appreciate it.

Rachel Shillcock for working your design magic throughout this book. I'm very grateful.

Lorraine Hamilton for not allowing me to give up.

Hannah Branton for all the daily phone calls. Everyone needs an accountability partner like you. I'm glad you're mine.

Lucy Chadwick for being a genius at problem solving and project management.

For mum for always helping me out. Without you I would never have achieved anything.

And to Dave for saying the right things when I needed them most and for always keeping me on the bus.

IMAGE CREDITS

Page 15, 43, 127 and 184 – Images by ananaline / Shutterstock

Interior Design by Rachel Shillcock

Printed in Poland
by Amazon Fulfillment
Poland Sp. z o.o., Wrocław